First published in Great Britain in 2016 by A Way With Media Ltd, Shrewsbury, SY3 7LN.

Copyright © Jonathan Smith 2016.

The right of Jonathan Smith to be identified as the author of this work has been asserted

by him in accordance with the Copyright, Designs and Patents Act 1988.

A CIP catalogue record for this book is available from the British Library.

ISBN 978-1-910-469-040

Writer and editor: Carl Jones

Editorial production/design: David Briggs

Publisher: Andy Richardson

Printed and bound by 1010 Printing International Ltd, China.

www.awaywithmedia.com

I dedicate this book to my family – wife
Ruth, daughters Rosalea, Enya, and
Alanya, and my parents. They help me
remember where I have come from and
are always by my side.

Jonathan

THE BEGINNER'S GUIDE TO ORGANISING AN EVENT

SAFELY

"I have a good friend called Chris who is a psychotherapist and he tells me: 'The more you are able to let go of the control, the more you are in control'. Remember, there is only one of you. Share the event and the workload and your event is more likely to be a success."

Special thanks to Carl Jones,
David Briggs and Andy Richardson

"The biggest fragility in a project is often just the inability to be able to explain to people why you are doing it, when you're going to do it, and what's going to happen..."

Lord Sebastian Coe, chairman of the London Olympic Games organising committee, speaking in November 2012

FOREWORD

So, you're thinking of organising an event, are you?

A fairly small-scale street party for the neighbours, perhaps, a bustling village fete, or a charity fundraiser?

No? Well how about something slightly larger, like a music or comedy night at the local town hall, an outdoor food and drink festival, or a corporate networking bash, with champagne and canapes.

Still not big enough for you? Push the boat out all the way then, and lay on a massive open-air rock concert, an air display, or a family-friendly activity day drawing people from far and wide.

The point is this; it doesn't matter whether your event is a low-key get-together for friends and family, or a giant festival drawing in tens of thousands of frenzied fans, the secret to success is the same . . . proper planning.

A well-planned event is a safe and successful event. In this jargon-free book, you'll learn from the people who have been there and done it, and pick up top tips to avoid the most common problems and pitfalls.

From the earliest planning stages, through budgeting, safety and risk management this is a step-by-step guide to organising the perfect event for maximum impact, with the minimum of stress.

Contents

chapters

case studies

INTRODUCING JONATHAN

OK, I know what you're thinking . . . Jonathan who? What qualifies this bloke you probably don't know from Adam to tell you how to set up and run your event?

Well, I'm not pretending that I've been everywhere, done everything, and seen it all, or that I have all of the answers, all of the time.

But if there's something that I don't know, I've been around in this business long enough to have a friend that does – that's what comes from working at the highest level of the events industry, all over the world.

For many years now, I've been in the privileged position of travelling the globe providing risk and safety consultancy advice to organisers of some of the biggest sports, business and leisure events around.

I lead something of an interesting life, advising promoters on how to organise their events efficiently, and – most importantly of all – safely.

I'm the man who has helped to keep the crowds safe at the Abu Dhabi Grand Prix, watched over fans at some of Britain's biggest music and motoring festivals, and made sure many smaller specialist events, like regional

food festivals, run without a hitch. Ask Jools Holland about the time I brought one of his concerts to a halt for half an hour, when there was a suspect package spotted by the stage. He never knew exactly what we were doing, at the time!

In my spare time, I also fly back and forth from Afghanistan, Iraq, Vietnam, Cambodia, Afghanistan, Libya and Egypt, and other hot-spots to advise on the removal of mines and share the knowledge I have gained, to keep people safe. The majority of these countries are working with mine clearance and UXO (unexploded ordinance) clearance and Mine Risk Education with various organisations or NGOs (Non-Government Organisations)

Life has also brought me into contact with some of the biggest event organisers in the world, and given me first-hand experience of best practice – thinking of every eventuality, to avoid a red-faced disaster.

My role is to identify potential problems, or 'residual risks', and to prevent them from happening and work behind the scenes to ensure that everything runs smoothly at a show, concert or display, come rain or shine.

It's all a far cry from the days when I started my career with the Local Authority in Wolverhampton, before entering the risk and safety business in the early 1990s.

I now run my own company, Online Safety Solutions, providing bespoke risk and safety advice all over the world – including some of the most troubled countries. I can be working on events where the capacity could be anything from 5,000 to 50,000. An enormous amount of planning and preparation is required when you are dealing with so many people in one place at the same time – not to mention cars, planes, horses, or other attractions which bring their own unique blend of challenges. In 2010, I was invited to learn about the work of the Mines Advisory Group (MAG), which helps to de-mine in some of the world's most challenging areas.

I met the CEO of MAG, Rob White. We just got talking and he

Clockwise from top left: Jonathan with Frankie Valli; flying with the Royal Navy; the firm's logo; the Abu Dhabi Grand Prix; with Rob White, former CEO of MAG.

invited me to look at what the group did.

I made my first visit to Iraq in 2011, and have also been back to the area since, working in locations such as Erbil, Chamchamel, Suleimanyah, and Kirkuk.

During this time, I have met many victims of uncontrolled detonations of mines and unexploded ordinance and I am only too happy to give my time to NGOs for free and fund my own trips. It makes you realise how lucky you are when you see such things in war-torn countries.

My job was not only to critically assess the way they de-mine, but holistically from the perspectives of security, transportation, office, safety and welfare. I am there to help them identify problems, way in advance.

I've been out to Vietnam and Libya to take on anti-mining work. I have also worked with several British Embassies, including the British Embassy in Cairo and the Egyptian Museum in Cairo, observing forensic examinations of Egyptian mummies and advising on security issues and fire safety in the underground crypts.

It's a remarkable lifestyle. One day I can be working in Qatar or Dubai, the next I could have been working in the USA or China, and the next I may pop up at a countryside food festival in the heart of England.

One of the best aspects of my work and profession is when our policies, procedures and safety management systems are tested and they work. At a food festival in Shrewsbury, for example, we had one medical emergency where a gentleman suffered a seizure. We got an ambulance onto the site immediately and he went to hospital. He wrote to the organisers later, to say thank you.

We've also had children go missing, which tends to happen quite regularly at festivals of a decent size. We've had as many as 20 lost children at a kids festival in one day but they were all found in a matter of minutes. It's wonderful when you take them back to their parents.

So, what's my motivation for this book? Quite simple – to make sure that, should situations like this arise, you are well prepared, and one step ahead of a potentially damaging problem or scenario.

In today's modern society, we are all coming under increasing commercial and ethical pressures to control and reduce risks.

When event organisers get it right, most visitors don't notice the hard work which has gone on behind the scenes. That's the dream scenario. But if they get it wrong, the risks and potential penalties have never been greater.

I wanted to combine the knowledge and experience gained over 25 years of working as a Risk and Safety Consultant with helpful tips and anecdotes from event organisers both in the UK and overseas.

Most importantly of all, I wanted to do it in a user-friendly way. There are many 'how to' publications out there, but they often make beginners and volunteers feel like they need a degree in event management to understand them.

The Beginner's Guide To Organising An Event – Safely is different. It's a down-to-earth guide to putting on a great show, drawing on my own experiences, and those of some of the biggest event organisers around.

So, whether you're looking to organise a village fete, or a rock gig for 40,000 fans, this will tell you almost everything you need to know. From crowd control to ticketing and risk and safety to providing emergency medical attention, I hope you'll come to view this book as a trusted friend that guides you through the process, safely and sensibly.

Jonathan Smith

WHY ORGANISE AN EVENT IN THE FIRST PLACE?

Let me start with a friendly word of warning, drawn from years of sometimes bitter experience.

A time will come, during the run-up to your event, when you will feel like you are banging your head against a brick wall.

Something will have gone wrong, completely out of the blue, and you'll think the world is conspiring against you. A voice in your head will quietly begin asking: "Why on earth did I think this was a good idea? What have I got myself into?"

Well, when that happens, just hold that thought.

Because you need to remember exactly what _was_ going through your mind back on that momentous day. Why _did_ you decide to roll up your sleeves and organise the event in the first place?

There will be many different reasons. You might want to raise cash for a good cause or charity; you may be doing it to encourage some community spirit and bring the locals together; or you could be taking a more pragmatic approach and viewing it as a money-making exercise.

One thing's for certain. Whatever the size and scale of your vision, you won't be able to do it on your own. It's vital that you pull together a group of like-minded fellow organisers, and that you are all crystal clear from the very outset about what it is you want to achieve.

So, when you have that panicked thought about why you've got yourself so involved, make sure you've got enough people around you to share the burdens and challenges.

Events – however large or small – can't be organised by just one person, so don't be either too proud, or too stubborn, to request or accept offers of help.

The larger your event, the more people you will need to help with the planning and organisation. And the broader their skills set, the better.

Never, ever underestimate how much time you will need to allow, to make sure everything is in place. In my opinion, it is impossible to start planning too early.

There's a well-worn phrase about risk and reward that comes to mind here – and it's certainly true that, the larger you aim, the more lucrative your event can potentially be.

TOP TIP: Never lose sight of why you got involved in the project in the first place – and use it as a reference point whenever the going gets tough.

But there's one particular area where no risks whatsoever can be taken and that is the health, safety and welfare of all within the event.

It would be foolish, irresponsible and frankly dangerous to leap into the process of organising any form of event without stopping to assess the risks.

Thinking about problems and scenarios before they happen and controlling or eliminating them to make sure they don't happen; that's what this event management business is really all about.

HERE'S A USEFUL SIX-POINT CHECKLIST FOR YOU.

IF YOU CAN ANSWER 'YES' TO ALL OF THESE QUESTIONS, THEN YOU'RE ON THE RIGHT LINES.

✓ Do you have a clear message about what your event is aiming to achieve – something which it will be easy to get across to potential visitors through publicity and marketing?

✓ Do you have evidence that your event is something that people will support, and that there is sufficient demand to cover organisational costs?

✓ Is your chosen venue capable of handling the maximum number of visitors you might attract – and are the relevant authorities happy for it to proceed?

✓ Will your event have longevity, by fostering close relations with supporters, community groups and partnerships within your supply chain?

✓ Does the proposed event have the support of those who live in the immediate vicinity?

✓ Do you have enough support stafff and volunteers available to shoulder the workload, without risking 'burn-out' as the big day looms?

ALL OF THOSE BOXES TICKED? GOOD. THEN KEEP YOUR MISSION STATEMENT AT THE FOREFRONT OF YOUR MIND, AND MOVE ONTO THE NEXT PHASE.

BECAUSE THERE'S A WHOLE LOT OF TALKING AND PLANNING TO BE DONE BEFORE THE ACTION CAN REALLY START...

HOW DO YOU START?

Imagine you're down the pub with a group of your mates. Now pretend that they're quizzing you about this event they have heard you are planning to organise.

Can you explain to them what it's all about, in just a couple of short, concise sentences?

This might sound like a ridiculous thing to say, but it is absolutely vital.

Because if you, the organiser are not crystal clear in your own mind about what you want to achieve, motivating others to jump on board your bandwagon will be tricky.

It's equally important that your event is easy to understand from a public relations point of view – when it comes to the big day, your audience will make a snap judgement about whether it's their cup of tea, before deciding whether to come along.

So, to the title of this chapter – how exactly do you start?

The mission statement

First and foremost, turn that chat with your mates in the pub into a mission statement, and write it down.

It might say, for example, something like: "My event will provide some much needed live entertainment in the community, and raise funds for charity."

Great starting point. Now, expand on that a little bit.

What sort of entertainment? Tea dancing for local pensioners, motor racing for petrolheads, fun and games for the whole family?

All of these would attract a dramatically different type of audience, impact on the size and nature of venue you might use – and could even dictate the time of year that your event would best be held.

And if you're raising funds for charity, which cause are you supporting, and why? Make sure it is relevant to your audience, and that you can explain, if challenged, why it was chosen.

Set yourself some key goals. What exactly do you want your event to accomplish? Bring in record-breaking crowds? Energise the local community? Become an annual fixture on the calendar? Raise the profile of a cause or campaign? Or simply to just raise as much money as possible?

Strength in numbers

It's crucial that you are able to gather a tight-knit band of volunteers to help with your campaign.

If you've pitched it right, and your mission statement is clear, and motivational, they shouldn't be too difficult to find.

Good team members with different skills are a necessity to the success of any event – particularly if you're organising it from scratch, for the first time.

From preparing schedules and budgets, to making invites and posters, manning the turnstiles, and helping with the less glamorous tasks like cleaning up afterwards, volunteers will help you to get things done.

Make sure you keep your key team members and volunteers up to speed with the planning of your event, and don't be afraid to delegate.

Collaboration will make your job easier, and make your support staff and volunteers feel more wanted, and appreciated.

And when you do ask people for their help, be clear and frank with them from the outset about exactly what is expected of them. You may be expecting them to dedicate much more time to your event than they have to give – finding this out when you are too far down the road can cause organisational mayhem. Not to mention bad feeling where none should exist!

TOP TIP: Make sure everyone can buy into your mission statement – and that doesn't just mean you and your fellow organisers, but your potential audience too.

The practicalities

Who do you want to come to the event – is it targeted quite specifically by either age or niche interest, or will there be activities for a range of different people? It's important to make sure you are crystal clear on this point, to ensure that the attractions are the right match for the audience.

How many people are you catering for? You need to have both a minimum and maximum figure in your head, to ensure you have the right facilities.

Will admission be free, or will there be a charge? And if you are charging for admission, how do you pitch the ticket prices, and when and where will they be on sale? Sometimes, it's worth offering discounted advance ticket sales, as this gives you an early indicator about the level of interest which exists out there for your event.

And remember, the bigger the event, the more people you will need to plan and organise on the day itself, and the more time you will need give yourself to plan and prepare.

Think about logistics. Will people be coming to your event by car or on foot? If it's by car, what will parking be like? Are there enough entry and exit points at your venue to keep the flow of traffic smooth?

It may be that Local Authorities (Safety Advisory Groups) will need to be informed formally. Make sure you've factored this in too.

With most events, particularly if you are expecting guests in the thousands, you will have to notify the Local Authority as a legal requirement. They will then disseminate the information to other organisations like the emergency services and hospitals, and this may require further discussion. More on all of that a bit later…

Meanwhile, what about accessibility on site for those with mobility problems? Does your chosen venue meet statutory legislation which is so important when public gatherings are held?

The list goes on. Will there be sufficient toilet facilities? What sort of first aid cover will be needed? And if you're holding your event in the great outdoors, what if the increasingly unpredictable weather doesn't play ball?

It's important to sit down for a minute with your team and consider all eventualities. Is there any obstacle or potential problem that can be foreseen and prevented? Any special guests that need to be accommodated? Any exceptions that need to be made?

Ah, we're back to that 'P' word again. Planning is the route to your peace of mind.

Case Study

V FESTIVAL

Every August since 1996, V Festival has been held across two stately parks for one epic cross-country weekend of live music.

It takes place simultaneously at Hylands Park in Chelmsford, and at Weston Park on the Staffordshire and Shropshire border.

World-class acts take to the stage at one venue on the Saturday, then move to the other on the Sunday.

When you're hosting an event which attracts such large crowds, it's vital to ensure that they arrive at the showground as prepared as possible.

That's why there is a comprehensive 'frequently asked questions' section on the V Festival website, to help minimise inconvenience.

It looks at questions like 'Can I charge my mobile phone at V Festival' – vital for the age and demographic of the audience – and what to do if tickets or wristbands get lost.

Many people choose to camp at V Festival, and there is advice about the size of camping pitches, and whether there are any restrictions on the size of tent you can pitch. You can't rent a tent at V, but they do offer a 'V Style luxury campsite'.

Camping stoves can be a health and safety accident waiting to happen at a public event, so V makes it very clear that no gas or LPG stoves are permitted – only small portable barbecue trays.

And they also tackle the issue of age restrictions, pointing out that children under 5 are not permitted, and anyone under 16 must be accompanied by an adult.

V Festival offers free drinking water from standpipes in the arena, and invites guests to bring refillable plastic containers. It doesn't allow visitors to bring any alcohol into the arena, and there is a strict 'no glass' policy across the showgrounds.

We asked the organising team to take five minutes out of their busy

schedule to share some of the experiences – and biggest challenges – they have faced over the past two decades.

What was the biggest challenge in those early days?
"Working with Local Authorities on such large projects, we had their support but it was something so new to them. We also wanted to work to ensure the public in the areas close to our festival sites came to think of the festivals as their own. We've definitely achieved this."

Who did you turn to, for advice and support?
"Each other, V Festival is owned and operated by year round concert promoters each came with their own experience and ideas."

Looking back in hindsight, what was the biggest mistake you made?
"Probably getting too comfortable with our event and brand. We had a couple of difficult years in 2014 and 2015 with not selling out for the first time in many years. We're very pleased that this year (2016) is looking like we'll be in a sold out position again."

If you could have done anything differently in the planning stages, what would it have been?
"Nothing really, we've worked hard to create an amazing event, we now tweak things year on year to add to the experience for our customers.
The great thing that social media enables you to do are to listen to your audience."

If you could give a budding event organiser three top tips, what would they be?
Keep an open mind to feedback, you'll never stop learning.
Employ industry experts and build quality relationships with people you need to work with.
Consider work experience and asking people if you can shadow them until you find the type of event you want to organise.

RIGHT TIME, RIGHT PLACE

If the 'P' word – Planning – is the most important aspect of this whole book, then the 'T' word must come a close second.

Timing, you see, is absolutely vital when it comes to making your event a success.

If I had a ten pounds for the number of shattered event organisers who'd planned their football awards night months in advance, only to find it clashed with a major sporting event, I'd be onto a nice little earner.

Or the dance competition committee members who enthusiastically scheduled their big annual showpiece, only to find it clashed with the grand final of Strictly Come Dancing, and everyone with a love of ballroom or Latin remained glued to their TVs at home.

The result? Lots and lots of empty seats at an event you have worked so hard to create, and an overwhelming feeling of being, well . . . underwhelmed.

The moral of this little story is simple: always check the local community's events calendar, cross-check it with the big national and international milestones, and try to project yourself ahead to the big day, to imagine what other calls there may be on people's time and attention that could distract them from attending your event.

Deciding on the right time and place is the single most important thing you will have to do. Leave no stone unturned

when it comes to doing your homework and researching the potential competition, not to mention clogging up the infrastructure of your event and the surrounding highway as it clashes with a nearby event.

Your dream scenario is to find a time when everyone will be free, and a place that's not only a convenient location, but is somewhere you can afford to book . . . and, of course, which is available!

But what is the best time and place? Well, that largely depends on your target audience, and chances are, you'll have to make some concessions along the way.

It's highly unlikely that you will be able to fit in with absolutely everyone's plans – but the pure fact that you have taken your audience's lifestyle habits into account will give you the best chance of a successful event.

If you are hoping to draw in crowds of stay-at-home mums, for example, then holding an event during the day and in the local neighbourhood is going to be your best bet (not forgetting to lay on some possible childminding facilities at the venue, perhaps). These people won't want to travel too far, so bear in mind that your catchment area will be relatively small.

If your entertainment is targeted more towards students, however, then think about holding it on a weeknight, somewhere downtown. That's where young people are already likely to be, after all, so you won't be asking them to change their habits.

And then, of course, if it's a more general event designed to offer something for the whole family, well the chances are you will need to make it a weekend – a day when it's most likely that mum, dad and the kids are all in the same place at the same time.

TIMING IS ABSOLUTELY VITAL WHEN IT COMES TO MAKING YOUR EVENT A SUCCESS.

TOP TIP: Make sure your venue is flexible enough to cater for a range of eventualities – and check the local and national calendar to ensure you're not clashing with other important dates.

There are lots of basic issues to consider, to help ensure everything goes smoothly. For example:

Your venue should have good transport links, parking space nearby and – particularly if it's more than one day long, or people are being encouraged to drink alcohol - accommodation close by. Think where your audience is travelling from and try to make sure their route is clearly signposted to ensure their journey is, partially stress-free.

The size and capacity of a venue must be just right – too small and you risk overcrowding if it turns out to be more popular than expected. Too big, though, and there will be no atmosphere or buzz.

See if your chosen venue has hosted similar events before. Were they successful? Are your tickets prices similar? It's important not to price yourself out of the market. Be realistic about what people will pay.

Is there a contingency plan for bad weather? Picture how your event might work if there's a heatwave, or a torrential downpour. Could you cope? Is your venue adaptable enough? We have cancelled events through bad weather and moved the position of a stage at the last minute due to issues of ground stability following torrential rain.

Ask your chosen venue management if they have action plans from previous similar events, or a gallery of images that you can view. This is a good way of forming a picture in your mind which will help to ensure the format is going to match your expectations.

Contact the venue management you are thinking about using as soon as possible. They may be busier than you are! Popular locations are often booked up more than a year or two in advance as any wedding promotor will tell you.

It's important to take an hour or two to visit your chosen venue – ideally with a couple of other helpful pairs of eyes from your organising committee.

Check for parking, on site and off site, logistical routes into and out of the venue, are there clear routes for vehicles to provide the infrastructure to build the event, to all the various entrances and exit points of the venue. Look at areas where there may be access restrictions, overarching trees, low bridges on vehicle routes, weight bridges with vehicle weight restrictions. Make sure there are no time constraints.

Do doors or gates get locked at certain times, and are there any fire alarm tests or other periodic maintenance tasks scheduled which might clash with the arrangements and procedures for your event?

Does the site have good mobile phone coverage – given that the younger generation feel like a loss of signal is akin to having their right arm cut off, this is an increasingly crucial consideration as pay tills and ticket verification often require a Wi-Fi signal.

And what about wi-fi? Is it available, and if so, worth giving to your visitors as part of their ticket price?

If you are planning a relatively small community event like a summer fair or a fete, a village hall or a school will usually suit your needs perfectly. If it's an event which is all about the community, it needs to be staged at a venue which is associated with the community.

Leave no stone unturned when it comes to asking questions. If there's the slightest nagging doubt, make sure you identify it with others and resolve the issue – there will be a reason why it's lingering in your mind.

Case Study

THE JOCKEY CLUB

"Detailed planning leads to the implementation of a successful event…" That's the view of Epsom Downs Racecourse's Matthew Worthington, who oversees some of the largest public sporting gatherings in Britain in his role as Regional Head of Operations for The Jockey Club. The Investec Derby Festival, for example, attracts well over 100,000 people to the historic racecourse on the Epsom Downs in Surrey.

And when you are channeling so many people in and out of a venue in such a short space of time, organisation and planning are absolutely essential.

The weekend includes a ladies' day on the Friday, before the main event – the greatest flat race in the world – takes place on the Saturday. It has grown into the largest sporting event in Europe.

There is live music to organise, market stalls, funfairs, hospitality packages, plus admission to six different enclosure areas around the course, and the whole event involves between 600 and 700 staff.

And when such a large crowd is brought together in one place, the responsibilities

for ensuring watertight security against the threat of a terror attack are enormous. No stone can be left unturned.

So how does the team approach the whole event? Above all, Daniel Cooper, one of the racecourse event managers says it is vital to remain level-headed, organised, and ensure that you have the right people doing the right jobs.

"Always being level-headed is crucial," he says. "As an event organiser, you will meet people, clients and contractors from all walks of life. This mix of people will be either useful, kind and helpful or challenging, unhappy or indecisive.

"As an event organiser it is up to you to manage this mix of people and find the best out of every situation."

Thinking one step ahead is vital too. Daniel says: "All of your actions will lead to further repercussions and it is up to an effective event organiser to think this through quickly, often on your feet to ensure all aspects are considered before making a decision."

He continues: "Be thankful and considerate. Not everyone is your friend, but everyone can help you with your event so make your staff feel valued and take on feedback they provide as they will ultimately be representing your values during the event."

For the Derby weekend at Epsom, build-up traditionally begins around four weeks beforehand, with the site breakdown continuing up to a fortnight after the final race has been run.

And the overall planning of the event is a 12-month process . . . in other words, it begins immediately after each Derby is complete. For 2016, however – the Queen's 90th birthday year – Epsom was planning its very special Derby for a whole decade!

The debrief from each event can last as long as four months – however smoothly Derby weekend may have gone, The Jockey Club are conscious that there's always something to learn; something to improve on.

Keeping visitors informed online is a crucial ingredient on the smooth running of Derby weekend. For example, the Epsom website addresses issues about the best public transport links, where to buy food and drink, and whether dogs are allowed.

It also clarifies the situation on whether visitors are allowed to have a barbecue on site (in case you were wondering, they are strictly forbidden in all enclosures including The Hill due to their proximity to the track). Meeting points, cashpoints, facilities for disabled customers, rules and regulations on picnics . . . all of these topics and more are spelled out clearly on the website, keeping customers briefed before they begin their journey, and helping to minimise potential disruption.

"Not everyone is your friend, but everyone can help you with your event so make your staff feel valued and take on feedback they provide as they will ultimately be representing your values during the event."

Daniel Cooper

THE BUSINESS PLAN

When you are investing so much of your own time in organising an event, the one thing you don't want to do is lose money. Breaking even (at the very least if it's the very first time you have dipped your toe into the water) should be your absolute minimum objective.

But you will only achieve this if you have covered every eventuality, and accounted for every last penny you will have to spend.

That means creating a solid, easy-to-follow business plan – and taking your time pulling it together.

I know it can often by the dull, tedious part of the job, but regardless of the scale, age or history of your event, a sound business plan is an essential tool. It needs to fulfil four key objectives:

Communicate the vision, the purpose and the benefit of your event to all members of your team

Show you how much money is going to be needed – and precisely what it will be needed for

Help you allocate and plan your resources, and develop an organisational structure

Assist in measuring your event's progress, and its success

Your business plan – just like the mission statement which we discussed earlier – needs to spell out the big vision, and what your event is ultimately aiming to achieve.

It needs to list all the key stakeholders, organisers, support staff and volunteers, utilising their experience and relevant track record.

It should also include a good old fashioned SWOT analysis, identifying Strengths, Weaknesses, Opportunities and Threats.

And, remembering that soundbite from Lord Coe at the very start of this book, there should be a comprehensive marketing and communications strategy which lets people know the basics . . . exactly what your event is about, and why you're holding it.

You'll also need to identify staffing requirements, along with all the services and facilities needed on the day itself. That's particularly crucial, because if you've overlooked anything once the doors have opened, there's no time to put it right, or very little, to combat at source or as we say "fighting fire".

And, last but certainly not least, you need a risk and safety management strategy . . . plus contingency plans for the worst-case scenario. The sort of thing you hope you will never need. We'll be talking in much more detail about these later on.

Executive Summary

Keep this nice and concise. It just needs an overview of what your event is and why it is being held, where and when it is taking place, and who it is being aimed at.

It should also pinpoint the market you are seeking to attract – is it for families, teenagers, music fans, etc.

Most summaries would also include a brief run-down of the estimated income and expenditure of the event.

Who, what, where, when . . . and why?

If your event is in its first year, explain where the idea came from; consider whether there have been similar events in the local area – and if so, examine how successful they have been. Does it show there's a demand, or should the warning lights start flashing about too much competition?

Spell out precisely what kind of event you want to stage, and the sort of people it aims to attract. If there is a particular audience profile you are hoping to tap into, this is the place to include it, to make sure everyone on your team is on the same wavelength.

Many times, I've encountered event organisers or volunteers who have been throwing themselves enthusiastically into the task at hand for months, only to find – when it's too late – that they were all working towards slightly different end products. The result? Confusion, demoralisation, and a lack of clarity for the event itself.

It's important, too, to describe the involvement and benefits that your event's stakeholders should expect . . . people like partners, public funders, sponsors, host venues, or community groups. Ask yourself whether you are meeting their objectives, as well as your own, because you might want to be signing them up again for next year. With your end goal at the forefront of your mind, outline your key objectives and how they will be delivered and developed. That means making a list of all the tasks, identifying who will lead each of them – and setting a structure to ensure progress is regularly monitored.

Write down a list of targets and objectives, and set clear timescales alongside each of them. Make sure your objectives are specific, relevant, and most importantly of all, realistically achievable. In other words, don't try to run before you can walk.

TOP TIP: Make sure that your business plan is geared up to make the most of your strengths and opportunities – but to also flag up potential threats, risks and weaknesses. Be flexible, and always open to ideas.

OPERATIONAL ISSUES

This is where you list the practical stuff in your business plan.

Facilities – do you need to draft in portable toilets, provide accommodation on or off site, offer catering, communication, car parking or camping areas?

Services – what services will be required and who will provide them: Do you need on-site medics, the police or fire service, traffic management systems, security guards? And what about a strategy for accommodating the media?

Showground – do you need extra power sources or generators for lighting, amplifiers etc? What about access for getting any heavy-duty delivery vehicle on and off the showground or venue – particularly if it's wet, and the grounds are muddy.

Keeping it legal – do you have the necessary public entertainment licences or permits, permission to sell alcohol, and all the insurances, policies and procedures, risk assessments and safe systems of work for the event, and the build-up and break down periods.

Reducing the risk – make sure you have a plan for managing and mitigating risks to the event. These could be physical risks such as accidents, financial risks through bad budgeting, or even reputational risks if the event doesn't go to plan, and your name is associated with it.

SWOT ANALYSIS

This is one of the most popular, and effective business tools for examining the strengths and weaknesses of your event plan, as well as identifying other opportunities, and pinpointing threats.

A good SWOT analysis will have lots of Strengths and Opportunities. A bad one will be top-heavy with Weaknesses and Threats.

It is best developed through brainstorming sessions with your fellow organisers. You know what that means? Yes, it's time to get the whiteboard and marker pens out!

The panel outlines some of the issues that event organisers might want to examine.

STRENGTHS

Are you offering something unique or different?

Are you the first, the biggest or the best value?

Are you meeting a known demand?

WEAKNESSES

Is there potential for weather to affect your plans?

Is there a risk of apathy from your audience?

Might the event cost more to stage than it earns back?

OPPORTUNITIES

Could you expand into new markets and attract different age groups?

Are there sponsors who might want to associate their brands with you?

Might others help you to promote the events?

THREATS

Clashes with other events taking place in the local area

Weather, once again!

Have you got your ticket pricing policy right?

Has the PR and marketing done its job and spread the word?

RULES AND REGULATIONS

Now I'm not saying this to put the frighteners on you, but if you get your risk and safety planning wrong and don't abide by event management rules and regulations (which can often run into many, many pages!), you could find yourself slapped with a costly lawsuit.

That's why it should always be the first thing to occupy your mind, once the event's business plan is in place.

Arranging a public event will in most circumstances be subject to the Health and Safety at Work etc Act 1974.

Other important areas of legislation are the Management of Health and Safety at Work Regulations 1999 and the Regulatory Reform (Fire Safety) Order 2005 which cover the risk assessment process.

There's also the Construction (Design and Management) Regulations 2015 which will apply where there is more than one contractor on site at any one time and this will usually cover the the build-up and break down period.

But alongside all of the applicable statutory legislation, it is important to use a common sense approach to risk and safety management too. There are many helpful and useful websites available, but the starting point should always be the Health and Safety Executive (HSE) or the HSE Managing Crowds Safely (The Purple Guide to Health, Safety and Welfare at Music and Other Events).

Your event may also need specific entertainment licences from the Local Authorities. If alcohol is being sold on site, well that's just another piece of paper you'll need, granting you permission.

It can often feel like there's no end to the number of boxes which need to be ticked, but don't start running scared.

The good news is that there are many experts, like myself, whose job it is to take care of all of these rules, regulations and safety standards, and to be on call at your event, keeping a close eye on proceedings from the background, to ensure all is going to plan.

Remember, it's you and your organising committee who are responsible for the safety of your support staff and fellow event organisers, volunteers and visitors.

When the Titanic went down over 100 years ago, the death toll was vast. Why? Because the cruise company had underestimated the number of lifeboats the ship would require when it hit that iceberg.

Instead of catering for the worst-case scenario, in those days before safety was at the forefront of people's minds, they'd taken a risk. They'd cut corners, and it almost sunk their business.

Never, ever cut corners. The Titanic's owners thought the disaster was unthinkable. Nothing should be deemed unthinkable when you're planning a public event.

If you're holding an event which could attract anywhere between, say, 500 and 5,000 people, you have to cater for the maximum – even though this is likely to increase your costs, it will still be a drop in the ocean compared with the bill you could face if you're found to be negligent.

So, you must ensure there are sufficient stewards, medical points, and toilet facilities, and much more.

You need to have a contingency plan in place in case there's a heatwave – bottled water available perhaps, places in the shade, and so on.

Conversely, if the heavens open and you are at Mother Nature's mercy outdoors, what if the ground turns into a quagmire with a risk of slips, trips, falls and broken bones, or the car park is under water and vehicles risk being stranded? Could you cope?

Of course, in the event of a fire, a missing person, or another major emergency, you need to prove you have systems in place which are swift, decisive and efficient, but also to prevent panic to your customers.

Every event will have slightly different priorities, but in general terms, this quick at-a-glance guide covers the key areas you might need to consider:

Fencing: Can they be opened to prevent a crush? Can the external site boundary be opened quickly in the unthinkable event that you have to evacuate the whole venue in the event of an emergency? Can it be opened to allow designated emergency vehicles to enter and exit – known as a designated 'blue light' route.

Stairways and ramps: Is your site accessible for all and compatible with the Disability Discrimination Act? It's important to think about the logistical implications for the event, and potential access restrictions.

Stewards: Do you have sufficient stewards to handle a crisis, and are they appropriately skilled and properly briefed?

Loudspeakers: Do you need a PA system to keep visitors briefed, and for use in the event of an emergency? Are you confident that your event will not breach noise pollution rules? The Local Authority may ask you to produce a Noise Mitigation Plan. It's important to make sure your PA system covers the entire perimeter, particularly important in the event of a lost child or an emergency announcement.

Seating and temporary structures: Certain seating and temporary planning structures should be suitably designed by a competent person. If factors such as wind loadings, point loadings or transferred loadings apply, then a Structural Engineer should be appointed. If there are elements of seating in a purpose-built grandstand, then again they need to be designed by a Structural Engineer. With temporary structures like inflatables, gazebos, bouncy castles etc, it is important to use a competent supplier to erect and operate them. Climatic conditions – particularly

TOP TIP: Picture the worst case scenario – everything that could possibly go wrong – then ask yourself: "Are we confident that we'd know what to do if it all happened at once?"

winds – can cause serious issues, and as an event organiser it is vital to monitor the weather before, during and at the end of an event if structures are not immediately disassembled. If the wind speed is high, or forecast is to be for high winds, then structures should be closed immediately and the surrounding areas suitably segregated. If a structure cannot be taken down or disassembled then additional supports may be required to ensure they are safe.

Electrical equipment: If electrical equipment is to be installed on site, then in most cases this should be only carried out by a competent and fully trained electrical engineer. As an event organiser, you must identify all of the services within your venue, both above and below ground. If you are erecting marquees then the last thing you would want is to put a steel rod or tent peg through a live underground service.

Entry and exit points: Are they sufficient to provide means of escape in an emergency, and properly signed for both pedestrians and vehicles? Again, remember you might need to accommodate a designated 'blue light route'.

Emergency services: Will your event need a doctor, paramedic, emergency medical technician or just qualified first aiders? This will be decided by your risk assessment for medical cover, along with the involvement from your Safety Advisory Group (SAG) committee who will then advise you. Generally, the bigger the event, the greater the risk - and the more support staff you will require.

Public conveniences: How many toilets and washbasins will you need? Do you need to think about baby-changing facilities, sanitary disposal bins, breastfeeding areas, or accessible WCs? When will they be emptied, cleaned and re-stocked? This all needs to be built into your risk assessment process.

Signposting: Do you need to put up signs on the surrounding roads to make the event easier to find? And if so, do you have permission to put them up from the Highways Authority? Might you need a Traffic Management Plan? Your local SAG committee will advise you on this.

Insurance: Do you need Public Liability Insurance in the event of an accident – or feel you ought to have it, for peace of mind? Is the venue adequately covered? Always ask for proof.

The first port of call for any questions should always be your Local Authority. Most have a standard procedure which involves notifying a local SAG about your plans, if they feel it is big enough to make a significant impact on the local area.

A brief synopsis of your event will be assessed by this group, potentially including the police, fire service, highways authorities and local hospitals, who will each decide whether they need to explore further.

It may be that with trained and competent fire marshals, security staff and stewards at strategic locations, the fire service is happy to keep its distance – but this will only be the case if you can show you have the correct resources and provisions to tackle a small fire, or prevent a fire from happening. We'll talk more about fire safety later.

By the same token, if you are planning a big event with possible crowd disruption or congestion, where there could be the risk of drink or drug-fuelled problems, the police may want to attend. If they do, you may be expected to pick up their bill.

As for the health service, if the nearest hospital or on-call ambulance is a long way from your venue – a particular concern if you are in a rural location – there will probably be requests to have comprehensive medical facilities on site. Again, this will be covered in your risk assessment.

I frequently end up having heated discussions with event organisers about the importance of having appropriately skilled people in the right places. It's no good just giving someone a hi-vis jacket and telling them they are a car park steward if they've never done it before, or been trained. This only leads to potential risks to the individuals . . . and ultimately to the event organisers too.

Nor is it any use giving a volunteer a pack of Band-Aid plasters or a tube of ointment and telling them they are the medical officer if they have no relevant experience.

Remember, these people are the public face of your event. Their effectiveness, and demeanour is directly linked to your reputation.

Legislation says your team has to meet what's known as the SKET standard – that's Skills, Knowledge, Experience and Training. In other words, they have to be competent to perform the job you've give them.

Case Study

THE KNIGHTS OF THE DAMNED

Hollywood stuntman Justin Pearson has appeared in some of the biggest film franchises in history . . . Star Wars, James Bond, Harry Potter, Fast & Furious, and Pirates of the Caribbean, to name just a few.

Having been in the movie-making business for nearly two decades, he's a man who knows more than a thing or two about risk, and making sure no stone is left unturned on the safety front.

And that last point, he says, is the most vital of all. A delay on a film set, caused by an injury to a stunt performer or an accident which may have been avoided, can cost the production company millions of pounds, not to mention wrecking your reputation, and making a lot of important people rather angry.

When he's not co-ordinating movie action, or rolling up his own sleeves

to bounce off cars, jump off buildings or get set on fire in the name of entertainment, Justin owns and commands a medieval jousting company called The Knights of the Damned.

It's a fusion of traditional horsemanship with a modern rock music soundtrack, inspired by the hit movie A Knight's Tale.

Sometimes, they are booked to appear as headline acts at country shows. On other occasions, though, the Knights of the Damned will organise their own full-blown family-friendly jousting events, with a show ring, craft stalls, and entertainment for people of all ages.

"When event organisers are interested in booking us, naturally the first thing that needs to be sorted is price," says Justin.

"They need to find out how much we are, to make sure it's within their budget. It sounds obvious, but it's important to get that crystal clear right from the start.

"If they want us, it's all confirmed – usually by email – and paperwork is sent out. We have our own contracts which are drafted, and we also send the event organiser our own publicity pack which includes a press release about us, and CDs full of pictures for advertising or promotion.

"We ask for a 25% deposit up front, and then the balance is paid at the event – so that's all that event organisers need to do, in terms of getting us committed.

"We send out a risk assessment, which covers what we will do in the arena, who can come into the arena while we are performing, and also our public liability insurance, which we have full cover for."

One of Justin's top tips is to make sure that, when you do book an act, they are encouraged to help promote your show by advertising their appearance on their own website or social media pages.

"We advertise all our appearance dates on our website, and we have a large Facebook following who travel around to watch us, so we're generating publicity for the organisers," Justin says.

"After all that is in place, we typically wouldn't hear from the organiser until two or three weeks before the event."

Bringing animals onto any site presents particular challenges. For example, the Knights of the Damned need a minimum space of 50m x 30m to perform their act, and ideally an area of 70m x 40m.

It has to be locked off around the arena, but with the crowd close enough to hear the hits and bangs, so they get the full effect of the show. All important considerations for an event planner when they are mapping out their site.

As you'd expect, there are many health and safety rules regarding animals moving within a showground – the Knights ask for a self-contained area of around 30m x 30m, close to the showground, which they will use as a holding pen and self-sufficient camping area.

"When we have to take horses back and forth from the ring, the organisers need to provide stewards to help with the trip," Justin says.

When it comes to organising his own event, rather than appearing at someone else's, Justin would typically start planning 12 months ahead.

"That's a timescale to be comfortable, I think, and not to put you under duress or stress. You need time to sort out the toilets, the catering, the tickets, and to book the entertainment – remember that the good acts will get booked up one or two years in advance.

"There are a lot of acts out there that are amateur or part time. We are a full time business, and I'd always recommend that event organisers make sure they know what they are booking, because it will be reflected in the standard of the entertainment.

"Your entertainment will make or break your show, as well as the catering."

The weather is, of course, the number one risk for any outdoor event. Justin says he looked at insurance to cover for a washout, but it's a very high cost.

"You ask yourself whether it's justifiable," he says. "The best thing to do is concentrate on getting traders on board, because they will pay a pitch fee. And if you can get your costs covered for staging the event by traders, then any ticket money which you take on the gate is clear profit.

"You might not guarantee that initially, because an event takes a bit of time to establish, but that is the ideal scenario."

Justin believes that venue choice is less crucial than the PR and marketing.

"You can put on the best event in the world, but if people don't know it's there, no-one will come. It's all about advertising." Justin Pearson

"You can put on the best event in the world in the most beautiful place, but if people don't know it's there, no-one will come. It's all about advertising. You need seven or eight different streams of marketing.

"We use things such as posters, press releases, social media, and other stunts. For example, we have a knight on a horse going round town centres with jesters, handing out leaflets on the weekends prior to the event – above all else, when you commit to organising an event, you need to be switched on with your advertising and marketing."

FIVE PHASES OF EVENT PLANNIN

The planning of a well-choreographed event can be broadly broken down into five stages.

First comes the **BUILD-UP** when all the groundwork is done on selecting the right venue, picking the best date, and choosing the appropriate number of skilled people to help out, both volunteers and paid staff.

This is the time when you'll have compiled a business plan, mapped out a budget, and gone through the full list of contracted-out services that you will need to call upon to make your event a success.

Consider whether you have mapped out your venue sensibly, and that there are not going to be any bottlenecks either for cars and pedestrians

entering the site on the day, or contractors delivering equipment or services beforehand.

Are any of your attractions timed to peak at a particular moment during the event? If there are demonstrations or live performances, space them out around the site, and try to stagger their timings too. I know that British people are the best queue-formers in the world, but that doesn't mean we enjoy doing it…!

Second is what is often termed the **LOaD-in** Once you've pinpointed what you will need in the way of fencing, barriers, staging, electrics, toilet facilities and public address systems – and checked that they are both available, and within your budget – you have to work out the logistics of getting them safely set up.

How long will it take? Where is the equipment coming from? Do the contractors require any heavy-lifting assistance or access-all-areas security passes?

This can sometimes involve very tight turnarounds. Make sure you have a good grasp on the earliest time that you will be given access to your venue. If there's a lot of pyrotechnic equipment to set up, and the venue is hosting another event the night before, you could be in trouble.

Do you need any kind of security on site before your event, in case valuable equipment is to be left there overnight? It's worth checking insurance policies – both for yourself, your venue, and any of your suppliers.

Thirdly, we have **SHOWtIME** – the day of the event itself. Who will be on site to man the ticket offices, car parks, entry and exit points? When and where will the first aid services be based? How will emergency procedures be communicated to your team on site – and from them, to the visitors in the event of a problem?

This is the day when you will need to have eyes in the back

of your head. You need a comprehensive inventory of all the people you will need on site, and make sure they are issued with the appropriate security passes, identification passes if applicable or just wristbands. The sourcing and printing of these should have formed part of your build-up discussions.

It is often best to allocate an event safety manager, or sub-group, to take responsibility for logistics on the day of the event itself. Don't be afraid to invite members of the emergency services, or Local Authorities, to join this team if you feel it may be appropriate. They will often welcome the opportunity to provide some input from a different perspective.

Next we have the **LOaD-OUt** The same sort of logistics have to be considered in reverse – how much time do you have to clear the site, and what needs to be done to guarantee safe removal of equipment and support services.

Ahead of both the load-in and load-out, you should have requested copies of health and safety policies and procedures, risk assessments, insurances and any required training certification from any contractor who will be entering your venue.

It's also a good idea to have a basic set of your own site safety procedures and a site induction. This will be required if your event comes under the Construction (Design and Management) Regulations 2015.

If any members of Local Authority, SAG Committee

TOP TIP: Map out exactly what will be happening on the day of your event – looking at a site design will often help to highlight any potential bottlenecks, or access issues.

or council officials want to check out the running of your event, it's precisely this kind of detail that they will pick up on.

And finally comes what is termed as the **BREAKDOWN** – when the contractors have taken their equipment away, you have to make sure you restore the venue to the condition in which you found it. That means making sure all rubbish bins are emptied, which can be a mammoth task in its own right.

If you've ever been to the V Festival on the morning after the final night, you'll be familiar with the sight of a seemingly endless sea of abandoned tents and camping kit – drowned in unthinkable piles of garbage.

In the case of V Festival, organisers have turned a potentially daunting challenge into a charity fundraising opportunity which has raised several million pounds, not to mention creating a great deal of goodwill.

Hundreds of volunteers, from organisations like local Rotary Clubs, collect up the unwanted ground sheets, sleeping bags, chairs and wellies and send them off to an organisation called International Aid Trust.

From there, volunteers on community service programmes clean them up and store them until they're needed to be shipped out to disaster zones struck by such things as hurricanes or earthquakes.

It's a win-win situation – the charity gains a precious resource it could otherwise never afford, and a potentially massive headache for the event organiser is eased.

Consider whether any of your inconvenient leftovers might be viewed as treasure by another local cause; inviting them in to help themselves could help make the event breakdown far less tedious . . . and if we're being cynical, it won't do your PR any harm either!

REMEMBER:

BUILD-UP

LOAD-IN

SHOWTIME

LOAD-OUT

BREAKDOWN

Case Study

GRANDSLAM MUSIC TOUR

The event specialists at Liz Hobbs Group Limited are the driving force behind the Grandslam tour, which kicked off by legendary British music group Madness.

It took in a host of outdoor locations, including football clubs, cricket clubs and racecourses.

In total, the Grandslam tour comprised of 21 events from 29th May to 26th September 2015, offering concert-goers the unique experience of an outdoor event with a festival vibe.

The first Grandslam featured Madness, and the aim each year is to increase the number of Grandslams, each featuring a different artist. By having these at different times of the year, it allows sporting venues to utilise their venues during their down time when the venues would not otherwise be used.

Liz Hobbs Group Limited are a creative bunch, committed to delivering amazing events that bring people together.

They create inspiring event packages, from small exclusive gatherings to 30,000 capacity rock concerts, working with some of the world's greatest venues and artists, combining music and sport.

The team have over 20 years of experience in event production, event management, stage and lighting design, organising tours, marketing and PR.

Liz says: "The biggest challenge was deciding which band to use for the launch of this new event. We wanted an artist who were a household name and who would embody everything that Grandslam stood for.

"They needed to be unique and really bring the party to the venues. Our next challenge is to ensure that the artists who follow understand and embrace the concept and the Grandslam vibe!

"I trust my team implicitly and we spent many months discussing the concept and looking at any potential challenges we may face, in producing a ground-breaking event and at many venues that had never staged an event before, let alone of this enormity!

"We worked with the band, management and agency to ensure that the event would meet all everyone's requirements. We wanted this to be something that people talked about for the whole year and they could look forward then to the next Grandslam.

"My parents are always a fantastic sounding board too. I always speak with them whenever I have a new idea as I know they will be honest with me, and often point out when I've taken leave of my senses!

"Transparency means you can spot any challenges hopefully before they become a problem and solve them together and this was truly a team effort."

Looking back in hindsight, would Liz have done anything differently?

"I try not to regret anything I do, whether good or not so good. I think you always learn from everything you undertake. Something which you may have considered to be a mistake at the time may stop you from making a far bigger mistake in the future.

"As a team we always do post-event analysis and Grandslam was no different. We were 100% honest with what worked well and what we would do differently next time.

"Accepting that you can always do something better in the future means that you are open to change and are adaptable. This is what makes a champion in sport and I believe a successful business too."

Liz continues: "As this was the first tour of its kind in the UK I don't think there was anything that we could have done differently with planning.

"Normally the planning stage is where you do your research and development, which also allows you to look at similar past events and use them as your potential template. As nothing like this had ever been done before it was impossible to look at other events and plan in this way.

"The only thing I would say about planning is to ensure that every stakeholder is bought into the plan at all stages, right from the beginning as this means everyone is on the same page. It helps to avoid any misunderstandings later in the process."

If Liz could give a budding event organiser three top tips, what would they be?

Don't be afraid to employ people better than you in specific areas. You're still the entrepreneur. They'll help you grow so much faster.

Trust your gut instinct; it's rarely wrong if you really listen.

Keep the emotion out of what is a business decision; you'll get better results sooner.

"Transparency means you can spot any challenges hopefully before they become a problem and solve them together and this was truly a team effort."

Liz Hobbs

Dealing With The Authorities

If your event is going to have any kind of impact on the surrounding area – however large or small – you'll need to notify your Local Authority. And it's always wise to keep local residents in the loop too.

Ideally, the authority will expect at least 12 weeks' notice, to give them time to inform other interested parties,or to find out more information, some Local Authorities will insist you will have to submit an initial form.

So, what are the areas that the enforcing authority and SAG Committee will be keen to know and find out more about your event? They may want to know what type of event you are arranging, the anticipated numbers, your audience profile, where and when the event will take place and they may also want to know whether you are requesting road closures.

They will probably want to see an Event Safety Management Plan. This will be dependent upon the size of your event. They may also wish to see your risk assessments including your Fire Risk Assessment and if your event is large enough, a Traffic Management Plan, a Temporary Demountable Structure Policy, a Severe Weather Management Policy, a Lost and Found Child Policy, a Drug and Alcohol Policy, a Campsite or Camping Policy and finally a an Emergency Contingency Plan. The aforementioned can be quite substantial documents and you may therefore need help in this area, SAG Committees generally want assurance within your documents that are

produced and implemented for your event.

Any information which you supply to the Local Authority will be passed on to the SAG Committees, including the police, fire, ambulance, highways, etc.

But it won't be circulated to any other third parties without your prior consent.

It may be that you require what's called a Temporary Event Notice to be issued, before your event can go ahead. This is usually only relevant if you are planning to sell or supply alcohol, provide live entertainment, or are looking to sell late night refreshments to the public.

It's important to remember that simply alerting the Local Authority to your plans does not absolve you, the event organiser, of ultimate responsibility for the safety of your event. The buck, the retained liabilities and responsibilities stops with you, especially under the judicial system in the UK.

If you're anxious to make sure you are playing by all of the rules, the Health and Safety Executive offers comprehensive advice on running events safely and it's worth taking a look at their website to make sure you've not overlooked any of the most crucial issues. The HSE's 'Purple Guide' is considered to be the bible for event organisers.

The emergency services will require risk assessments and detailed maps on your procedures for blue lights routes, fire plans, safety plans.

It is vital that your event staff, stewards, contractors, supply chain and volunteers are aware of the procedures you have implemented for your event to run safely.

The Local Authority departments which are likely to give your event the closest attention are the Environmental Health Department and the Emergency Planning Department.

It may be that they decide residents in the immediate area

need to be notified in advance. If so, they will usually issue a letter, or leaflet, outlining the date, time and nature of the event, including details of a named person to contact in the event that a complaint is to be made, or clarification needed.

You might want to consider a gesture to local people who could be inconvenienced by your event, offering free tickets to everyone within, say, a two-mile radius. It shows you are taking their feelings into account.

If your event is in, or close to a largely residential area, the Environmental or Public Protection Officers will want to ensure that any loud music, or amplified effects, will finish no later than the times specified by either the licence or authorisation requirements.

They may order that music from other sources, such as food retailers or fairground rides, may not permitted at all, and if you are planning to use fireworks or any other kind of pyrotechnics, this can't be done without their prior consent.

The word 'pyrotechnics' still sends something of a shiver down my spine. A few years back, I was working at an event involving music, fireworks and a fly-past from a Royal Navy Squirrel and a Gazelle helicopter.

The pyros were supposed to go off after the helicopters had flown past, but for some reason, four rockets went up right in front of the crowd line, just as the helicopters were passing over!

This kind of thing is taken very seriously, and I was summoned to see the Wing Commander to explain what went wrong. The investigation took nearly seven months, but it had been videoed, so we were able to piece it all together.

It turned out that there was a communication breakdown with the people letting off the fireworks – remember that in the world of risk and safety management, communication to all required parties is vital.

On the back of some high-profile accidents at flying shows in recent years, aerial displays are no longer permitted to take place over large crowds of people.

For example, the Cosford Air Show, one of the UK's largest and most popular annual aviation events, has revealed how it now faces tighter safety regulations.

Measures include "enhancing" the experience, skill and health that display pilots must demonstrate before being allowed in the air.

The regulators, the Civil Aviation Authority (CAA) has also toughened the safety checks, altered the display lines and criteria, heights of the display, the types of manoeuvres, and the crowd line to the display area. All of the factors should be carried out within an enhanced risk assessment for the display which the CAA

TOP TIP: Give yourself plenty of time to apply for all the licences and permissions you will need – particularly if you are planning live music, or firework displays.

will need to approve before they grant the permission. On all the aerial displays you will need an FDD (Flight Display Director) who can coordinate the display with the pilots and the ATC (Airport Traffic Control).

IT'S IMPORTANT TO REMEMBER THAT SIMPLY ALERTING THE LOCAL AUTHORITY TO YOUR PLANS DOES NOT ABSOLVE YOU, THE EVENT ORGANISER, OF ULTIMATE RESPONSIBILITY FOR THE SAFETY OF YOUR EVENT.

Case Study

JIGSAW MEDICAL SERVICES

Jigsaw Medical works with some of the biggest brand names in the business. Its clients include Virgin, Sky, ITV, BBC, McDonald's, Veolia, and Moneysupermarket.com . . . to name just a few.

One of its four divisions specialises in providing ambulance services, event medical cover and cover for TV and film units, while another is tailored towards special one-off projects, offerings medical training and staff for close protection, hostile, or remote environments.

Most recently, Jonathan Smith worked with Jigsaw Medical Services at the International Horse Show weekend, in Liverpool.

Richard McManus, director of clinical services at Jigsaw and also a trained paramedic, offers this advice to event organisers:

"Firstly, event organisers should only use Care Quality Commission registered medical companies; this ensures that the company work to a highly regulated set criteria for diagnosing, treating and transporting injured people to hospital or around an event site.

"While the Care Quality Commission (CQC) does not cover event medical companies at present, this is due to change in the near future and the event organiser should consider this when receiving quotations and considering medical cover.

"It is never too early to appoint a medical provider to be involved in your event planning process and guide you through the correct cover. This also helps to avoid escalating costs and will add medical cover into your budget early on.

"Large events will normally engage with a medical provider 12 months prior to the actual event or start immediately after the previous year's event has finished.

"This is great for implementing positive and negative feedback into the next event planning process."

So, what should a good event medical company do?

Richard says: "They will assign the event organiser with a point of contact who will be able to advise what safe levels of medical equipment and cover is required.

"The levels of medical cover should be checked against an industry guide and not the previous year's cover or previous medical providers level of cover."

Some examples of this include:

The Purple Guide to Health, Safety and Welfare at Music and Other Events
Guide to safety at sporting grounds.
UK athletics road race medical requirements.
British Triathlon Rule book

Richard says: "A number of events will fall outside of these guidelines and a mixture of publications should be used to achieve a safe level of medical cover.

"This is particular useful for extreme sports events which may not be regulated but involve swimming, deep water, running and mass participation.

"If the medical requirements are not clear, then consult the local NHS Emergency Planning Team/ Resilience Team for further guidance or to confirm the levels are what they would expect."

A good detailed medical plan outlines levels of cover, skill levels of the medical team (for example, Doctor, Paramedic, Nurse, First Aider), as well as distance to the nearest hospital, key contact numbers on the day, medical risk assessment.

Richard adds: "A number of medical plans will also incorporate an operational plan which outlines how the medical cover will be operated on the day, logistical plan and other key information required on the day.

"The operational plan is often more useful for the medical team to work with on the day.

"A copy of the medical plan should be available at any safety advisory group meeting and also sent to the local NHS Ambulance Trust prior to the event."

He continues: "Costs for medical cover vary between companies and this can be greatly reduced by knowing exactly what level of cover you require, requesting quotes early and booking early with written confirmation. Ensure that planning, meetings, site visits and fuel mileage is added into the quote.

"Often event organisers will approach medical companies late in the day for their event and will have limited time to plan the correct medical cover and a limited budget.

"Often event organisers will ask for 'first aid' cover but this may not be the appropriate level and likewise not every event requires a doctor or paramedic."

KNOW WHO YOU NEED – AND WHAT THEY DO

Doctor: Registered with the General Medical Council and has experience in for the event. Request the doctor's GMC number

Paramedic: Registered with the Health Care Professions Council. Again, request an identification number

Nurse: Registered with the Nursing and Midwifery Council. Request NMC number

Emergency Medical Technician: Not a registered professional but will have had over four weeks of training to work at emergencies and treat a number of illnesses

First Person On Scene (FPOS): Normally someone who has undergone a five-day medical course to deal with medical emergencies and illnesses

First Aider: Normally involving a three-day course.

Richard says: "Consider if your event requires an event control and if it would be of benefit to have a medical representative in the event control to manage the medical resources.

"Often complaints about medical cover centre around delays in getting medical help to an injured person and having a link in an event control can reduce delays or help the event organiser monitor response to incident times.

"Should a serious incident happen at your event then it is best practice to have key people from medical, security, safety management and production in a central location to make decisions about if the event can continue or how to handle the incident effectively."

"It is never too early to appoint a medical provider to be involved in your event planning process and guide you through the correct cover. This also helps to avoid escalating costs and will add medical cover into your budget early on."

Richard McManus

A Licence To Thrill

Don't assume that, simply by hiring a venue, you will have all the licences you need for your event to go ahead legally.

The Event Planning Licensing Act spells out a series of specific requirements that you'll need for public entertainment, sporting events, or the sale of alcohol.

A Premises Licence will be required where any of the above activities are going to take place unless the event is very small, in which case a Temporary Events Notice (TENs) may be issued.

What's the difference? A Temporary Events Notice is for an event which lasts no more than 168 hours and has no more than 499 people attending at any one time (including all staff).

Bear in mind, though, that there are limits on the number of TENs that can be applied for.

Where alcohol is to be sold in connection with a premises licence there must be a Designated Premises Supervisor (DPS) named on the licence and you may need an Event Alcohol Policy, this may include the procedures for the "Challenge 25" policy and statutory requirements.

And when an event is pre-planned, you must have this licence available to hand over to the Local Authority at least 10 days before your event gets under way.

If you are playing live or recorded music at your event you are responsible for contacting the Performing Rights Society and arranging a permit.

It's wise to state what type of entertainment and music you are providing (live or recorded) clearly within your Event Safety Management Plan or Noise Mitigation Plan – transparency on these sorts of matters is always the best policy.

Last but not least, are there any Merchandising or Special Licensing certificates you may require?

It's vital that you do everything reasonably possible to ensure that nothing for sale at your event breaches any licence requirements, trading standards, copyright or trademark regulations.

If in doubt about whether or not a proposed merchandise stand should be registered or licensed, the licensing team at your Local Authority will be able to help.

A handful of events are exempt from licensing. These include:

Genuinely private functions

Live TV and radio broadcasts

Garden fetes and similar not-for-profit activities

Music or plays associated with religious services or meetings

Morris dancing, or similar

Entertainment on a moving vehicle

Case Study
SHROPSHIRE FESTIVALS

Beth Heath is the driving force behind a growing number of public events in the county of Shropshire. They include the Shrewsbury Food Festival, Shrewsbury Christmas event, Shropshire Kids Festival, and Telfood Feastival in Telford.

"I started my own company three years ago following a successful career in events over the past 12 years, as I wanted to stretch my creative event ideas," she says.

"The biggest challenge in those early days revolved around money, and getting people to believe in some of the more adventurous ideas!"

Shrewsbury Food Festival is a showcase of food and drink, with local craft, unsigned bands and family entertainment, which attracts around 25,000 people over two days in June. It was launched because Beth and her fellow organisers felt the town's exceptional food scene had been a well-kept-secret for too long. The festival also shines the spotlight on local charities.

"Shrewsbury has great producers, great restaurants and great independent retailers. Our festival aims to bring economic benefit to all in the food sector, particularly artisans," Beth says.

Telfood Feastival, in the nearby new town of Telford, is a similar themed event, held in July.

The aim of this one is to bring over 130 amazing food and drink producers together to showcase their artisan products, alongside a big music stage, free talks and demonstrations a free Big Top with circus skills for the kids and lots of hands on, educational and fun activities for the little ones.

So who did Beth turn to, for advice and support before setting off on her event organiser's journey?

"My husband has been amazingly supportive, and our poor friends have helped massively with babysitting and giving feedback on ideas, along with the exhibitors who are ever helpful with practical suggestions.

"Looking back in hindsight, the biggest mistake I made was not making the jump to 'do it alone' sooner – it's a huge gamble and scary financially but great fun."

If Beth could have done anything differently in the early planning stages, she's in no doubt what it would have been.

"To get more help sooner; I love crazy ideas but I definitely need sensible administration support to be more businesslike!"

To budding event organisers, she offers these top three tips:

Talk to all the people who would benefit from the event be it exhibitors or the target audience, they'll all have a perspective you've never considered.

Check and check again, I manage my entire business from 'to do' lists – never throw them away, they're invaluable to remind you of tiny details in the future.

Win the lottery . . . then all of your mad ideas can become a reality!

DON'T LET YOUR EVENT GO UP IN SMOKE . . .

It could be a discarded firework, Chinese lantern, exhaust manifolds on dry grass, faulty or untested electrical equipment, or it might begin with an overworked and overheating generator.

The possibilities of a fire breaking out at a public event are endless – particularly when you are bringing in so much portable equipment into a venue. And that's why a Fire Risk Assessment is absolutely vital.

Event organisers are under increasing commercial and ethical pressures to reduce and control risk. I spend a growing amount of my time providing risk and safety assistance to address statutory health and safety responsibilities – with fire risk audits forming a pivotal role.

No event, however large or small, should proceed without a Fire Risk Assessment.

It is imperative that this is only carried out by someone who is competent and can identify all of the potential residual hazards and implement the required control measures. This could be through fire safety engineering systems, or safety management systems, fire alarms and call points to the fire

marshals, fire extinguishers and the required signage.

When undertaking and compiling a Fire Risk Assessment for your event, follow the HSE Five-Step Risk Approach in accordance with the Management of Health and Safety at Work Regulations 1999 (see overleaf).

The objectives of a Fire Risk Assessment and the Fire Safety Procedures that you have implemented for your event should generally be following:

Create positive safety management systems to minimise risks

Provide and maintain a healthy and safe environment, systems of work, plant and equipment that are safe, as reasonably practicable

Fulfil all legal obligations imposed upon event organisers, and follow industry best practice

Safeguard the health and safety of the public, contractors and participants who could be affected by the activities of the event

Ensure that all those involved in your event receive adequate training in safe working methods, accident prevention and emergency procedures, applicable to the job they are being asked to do

Encourage active employee participation in risk and safety matters and maintain a high standard of awareness

Provide a mechanism to monitor the application of fire policy and procedures, and strive to continuously improve safety performance

It is a responsibility of the event organiser and their team to take all reasonable steps to ensure safe conditions.

The Fire Risk Assessment and the Fire Safety Procedures implemented for your event, and any subsequent changes made to it as your event planning evolves, need to be brought to the attention of all who could be affected.

That means all contractors, employees and others engaged within your event must be aware of their specific responsibilities for general safety and fire safety.

It is wise to check that all contracted non-employees have written, safe working practices, adopt industry best practice for controlling fire risks and co-operate with regards to the maintenance of safety standards.

Don't just assume they know what they are doing – check for yourself, and hunt down the paperwork to prove it.

Good planning, communication and co-operation, means a higher standard of health and safety for all who are involved.

All findings – however insignificant you think they might be – need to be recorded, and any deficiencies identified must be prioritised and rectified at the earliest opportunity.

Although event organisers of large-scale events have overall responsibility for fire safety matters, they often appoint external companies like mine to assist in the arrangements over fire safety, which includes a comprehensive fire risk assessment.

Whichever way you choose to go about it, the objective is the same – aiming to secure the health, safety and welfare of all those who participate and attend your event and to protect against any residual risks identified.

The Five-Step Approach

Management of Health and Safety at Work Regulations 1999.

1 Identify potential fire hazards

2 Decide who (employees, general public, participants, stewards, support staff etc) might be in danger, in the event of a fire and note their location

3 Evaluate the risks arising from the hazards and decide whether your existing fire precautions are adequate or whether more should be done to get rid of the hazard or to control the risk (e.g. by improving the fire precautions).

4 Record your findings and details of the action you took as a result. Inform all affected parties of the findings.

5 Keep the assessment under review and revise it after the event

IDENTIFYING FIRE SAFETY HAZARDS

The most common sources of fire at a public event are:

Smokers materials - cigarettes, matches and lighters

Radiant heat, car manifolds and exhausts against long dry grass

Pyrotechnics/Fireworks

Electrical equipment and plant

Deliberate ignition (arson and vandalism)

Lighting

Climatic conditions

If various items of cooking and catering equipment are to be used within your event, or if you are encouraging visitors to stay overnight at camping facilities, you must pay special attention the fuels which could be present on site . . . because silent killers could be at work.

Never underestimate how deadly carbon monoxide fumes can be within an enclosed structure. There have been many tragic fatalities from the effects of carbon monoxide poisoning due to someone having a barbeque within a tent or a confined space.

It's a reminder of how deadly fire and fumes can be.

As previously mentioned within this book, all electrical equipment should be suitably inspected by a competent person and in accordance with the item of plant or equipment manufacturer's recommendations and guidance.

A thorough electrical inspection needs to be undertaken by trained and competent electrical engineers, to make sure everything on site complies with the 17th Edition Electrical Regulations and the Electrical Safety Installations Regulations 1999.

This means all portable electrical equipment being visually inspected and proven to be compliant with recommendations for portable appliance testing (PAT). Any temporary electrical service supplies must be included in this audit.

The use of petrol generators should be discouraged wherever possible, in favour of diesel generators.

Gatherings of rubbish and debris are a common factor in a fire breaking out at events, so make sure you have a system in place for regular clearance to prevent build-up of combustible materials on and around the venue.

Sufficient numbers of rubbish bins need to be in place, and if you are expecting big crowds, you'll need to ensure they are regularly emptied by waste disposal contractors and disposed of in the correct manner.

All lamps, lanterns, lighting appliances and any other apparatus liable to become heated, whether under normal or abnormal conditions and liable to come into contact with combustible materials need to be fitted with suitable guard such as wire mesh – think of it as child-proofing.

Of course we hope that the worst won't happen, but if a

steward or the event organiser is informed of a fire during the event, would they then know what to do. Make sure they receive some basic training as a fire marshal and that they are aware of the procedures for fire and safety for the event.

And at last, but certainly not least . . . make sure your venue is equipped with the appropriate fire extinguishers, strategically sited, and that you have trained and competent fire marshals or stewards who are properly briefed on how to use them.

TOP TIP: Don't take risks with fire safety – make sure every item at your venue is properly tested, and that you have the correct fire safety procedures in place for your event.

WH Management Group (WHMG), a company I have worked closely with on many occasions, is involved in on-site security at around 130 leisure and entertainment events across the country

Its biggest challenge, it says, is getting first-time clients to understand the benefit of planning, preparation and expenditure on security and emergency cover.

Managing director Douglas Hinckley told me: "Event organisers need to plan, plan plan.

"Have an appropriate sized 'event control', even if that is just a single person at a desk with a map, emergency numbers, a radio and telephone.

"Make them record ALL incidents from burst pipes to major incidents. This will ensure a swifter and appropriate response as well as lessons for the following year.

"Budget control and do not rely on cash ticket sales to cover set up and contractor costs, and remember that accidents and incidents will happen anywhere. Do not rely on county emergency services apart from major incidents. Follow good practice and listen to experienced contractors."

Douglas says: "You cannot mitigate all risks, especially when the public and trade are concerned. But you can have suitable assets in place to deal with the incidents."

Opposite are some examples of accidents WHMG has dealt with over the years.

"An incident can be as simple as this one. This was a caravan fire caused by an electric kettle being placed on a gas hob, as they were the same colour and design."

"This one was a case of bad parking practice. No organisation, cables everywhere and this overheated as a later vehicle parked a tyre over a hook-up cable."

"This final picture was a lorry fire caused by an overheating extension lead under a duvet. Good spacing and on-site fire crew prevented the blaze spreading to other lorries."

Risk and Safety Management

You will hopefully have noticed from this book that I have an underlying message regarding risk and safety management when it comes to events. Given my profession, this is not unusual.

I am a firm believer, though, in a common sense risk management approach – this is something that the HSE has proactively endorsed and to which I wholly agree. It is something that I have been implementing for around 25 years now, and I will continue to do so.

When it comes to assessing risks at your event, apply the fundamental basics of common sense risk management and you will start well. Use them, as we Risk and Safety Consultants do, and apply the general principles of prevention; whenever and wherever possible:

Eliminate the risks associated with the event, whenever possible

Reduce the remaining risk, wherever possible

Control them; if they remain.

The process of risk assessment is a starting point for any event and will make your event in general, fairly compliant with various parts of associated legislation. Risk Assessments do not have to be an over complex document. They do however have to identify the risks associated with your event, by doing this you should be able identify the hazards and risks;

HAZARD

A Hazard is anything with the potential to cause harm to you or others

RISK

Risk is the potential of something happening that has the potential to cause harm to you or others

MANAGING HEALTH AND SAFETY

Managing health and safety for your event again doesn't have to be complicated, costly or time-consuming. In fact it's easier than you think. If you have taken reasonable steps to prevent accidents or harm to your support staff, volunteers or visitors then this will be a good start.

For many events, all that's required is a basic series of practical tasks, including your risk assessments, that would enable you as the event organisers to protect your support staff, volunteers or visitors from harm and at the same time protect the future success and growth of your event, good health and safety can be good business.

I remember watching recently a re-shown programme on BBC

Four which was called, 'Jet! When Britain Ruled the Skies' and it featured footage of the Farnborough Air Show in 1952.

During the air display a test pilot, John Derry was flying a DH110 and part of his flying display was to go adjacent to the spectators watching below.

Unfortunately the plane broke up at speed and it subsequently fatally injured both the pilot and the co-pilot.

The tragic breakup of the plane resulted in the engines falling into a hill where thousands of spectators were watching the display. The result was the death of 28 spectators and over 130 casualties. Once the injured and fatality injured had been removed from the air show, along with the plane's wreckage, the event went on.

Would we do this today? Of course not, for many reasons, we are accountable both morally and corporately on all our events and this should be reflected in your events.

I have seen too many accidents, incidents and, unfortunately fatalities to know the extent of loss, both for the event organisers and more so for the families of the people affected by the loss.

We have learned a lot since 1952, we continue to learn every day. I strive to make all of my events safe and by following the basic rules and procedures, assessing and continually evaluating the risks associated with your event, and by eliminating or controlling the risks, your event should be fairly safe.

Case Study

SOUTHWATER EVENT GROUP

Southwater Event Group owns The International Centre in Telford, one of the UK's largest conference and event venues with more than 15,000 square metres of space, just a couple of minutes off the M54 motorway.

Events manager Vikki Kennedy has spent well over a decade in the industry, starting out as a waitress in a busy conference and exhibition centre, becoming a wedding co-ordinator for hotels and then moving into event management.

She says: "Over the last five years there have been quite a few changes to regulations in the industry. For example, there's a lot more help and advice available to organisers these days from venue staff, the Association of Event Organisers, electronic guides, and health & safety consultants.

"Health and safety awareness has continued to increase - some of the changes to regulations have pushed for that.

"Organisers have also become much more conscious of cost, and events now have a bigger emphasis on technology, with even the smallest stands routinely having iPads and smart TVs."

Demonstrating you take your environmental responsibilities seriously is more important than ever, too. Vikki adds: "We get asked about our green credentials much more now.

"There is also a greater demand for locally sourced food and traceability with food suppliers – not to mention many more dietary requirements than five years ago."

So what, in Vikki's opinion, is the most important thing which an event

Some of the events that have been hosted by The International Centre in Telford

organiser has to consider?

"I'd say that it's the health and safety of all delegates, staff, contractors etc during the event build, open and breakdown.

"Alongside this would be the overall visitor experience, from how easy it is to get to the venue to what sort of food is on offer."

And the most common organisational or health and safety points which exhibitors and event organisers tend to overlook?

"Checking that companies they use are competent; just because they have a fancy website doesn't mean they're any good at their job (or occasionally, that they are even qualified to do it in the first place).

"Reading paperwork sent by the venue would also be included – things such as the venue e-guide, or the Construction (Design and Management) Regulations 2015.

"And then there's closing the event, and the breakdown – how to manage a hall full of exhibitors wanting to leave while the last few delegates are still chatting to stand holders, at the same time as the contractors want to get in to breakdown the stands."

Vikki says the International Centre has not had any serious problems during an event, other than factors completely out of anyone's control such as a power cut – which can happy to anyone, any time.

But she adds: "We do a lot of pre-event planning around issues such as parking high numbers of vehicles to try to avoid upsetting the local residents, plus delegate flow and queue management when we have large numbers expected.

"We also have a few events where there can be security threats, so we have teams available to deal with incidents that could arise and procedures in place to pull in more resources if required."

Location, she says, is extremely important to the success of an event. But she adds: "Don't be scared to take events to places outside the city centres.

"You retain the delegates because there isn't as much to distract them. There will be no premium price to pay, giving value for money, better experience and sometimes nicer staff (can you guess where I work!?)."

When it comes to raising the profile of an event, and spreading the word to maximise awareness and potential visitor numbers, Vikki's advice is to use the team at the venue.

"They usually have contacts with the council and local businesses which can put you in contact with other appropriate events that you could advertise at. And make sure you take full advantage of social media."

When Vikki holds her first meeting with a potential event organiser considering The International Centre in Telford, she would ask them for an overview of their event, a rough itinerary, and the profile of the visitors it is hoping to attract.

She'd also want to know about any catering ideas, the overall aim of the event, and would expect to get a rough guide over the size of space which will be required.

Finally, she would find out if the organiser had used any previous venues, and pinpoint any additional costs which may be incurred – making sure there are no last-minute financial shocks from the venue team.

"To anyone looking to organise an event for the first time, I'd advise them to consult experts about the health and safety side, to look into other events which could be similar, and to chat to venues – they have a wealth of information and ideas.

"I'd also urge them to investigate a venue's e-guide, which brings together guidance for achieving common standards of health, safety and operational planning, management and on-site conduct, and do their homework on industry regulations.

"Gets lots of quotes, ensure whoever you decide to work with is competent, and read the contracts thoroughly.

"Make sure you get prices at the time of enquiry or booking, so you don't get any shocks.

"It's usually the best time to negotiate because they'll want a signed contract from you - never assume something is free or included, even water on tables for a gala dinner, or a power socket for a laptop."

GETTING PEOPLE IN, AND GETTING PEOPLE OUT

Getting people on and off your site is one of the most important logistical challenges. Get it right, and people won't even acknowledge the hard work which will have doubtless gone into making everything run smoothly.

But get it wrong and . . . well, chances are folk will be moaning about it for months.

First and foremost, make sure that there are clearly marked and separate entrances and exits to your site for vehicles, and pedestrians, and that they're as far away from potential bottlenecks as possible.

Make sure too that you've considered what might happen if you have a snaking queue of people or cars, and that you won't be obstructing anyone's property, or causing hazards at access points or junctions. The last thing you want, if you're organising an event for the first time, is to get on the wrong side of the neighbours…

If you have a limit on the number of people that your event can accommodate, make sure the entrance is well stewarded and that you have a reliable method of head counting to prevent overcrowding.

Overcrowding should be considered within your event Fire Risk Assessment and your Fire Safety procedures.

Communication is particularly vital in this area, if you are marshaling more than one entry point.

If your event is indoors, you should have already completed a Fire Risk Assessment which will have included a figure on maximum occupancy, and considered emergency escape routes.

It's always worth checking to make sure you know how responsibility is divided between the venue owner and operator, and you and your event management team.

If your event is outdoors, I usually recommend that you have at least two pedestrian exits – as a general rule of thumb, they should allow you to evacuate your entire site in the event of an emergency in no more than seven or eight minutes.

Each exit should be at least 1.5 metres wide, clearly marked, and free from obstruction. An exit of this size will typically allow around 125 people to pass through every minute in the event of an emergency – so you can do the maths yourself from this, and work out how many you are likely to need. As an event organiser you will need to consider getting an emergency vehicle into your site – the "blue light" route again. This will be within clearly defined and accessible routes.

Car parks should be positioned well away from pedestrian access areas, and again clearly signposted with your suitable stewards.

Remember also that your event stewards will need looking after also, the correct PPE (Personal Protective Equipment) this could be a high visibility vest or jacket, sun cream if you are lucky enough to have good weather and water and suitable rest breaks. Again this should be considered within the risk assessment for your event.

It's vital, when visitors are coming onto your site, that car parks are efficiently stewarded – make sure they are designed in a way which prevents vehicles having to reverse, where possible, as this is one of the guaranteed problem points at hometime.

One of the clearest ways to do this, especially for SAG Committees is to implement a Traffic Management Plan (TMP) to consider how your visitors' journeys can be managed in the most effective way, causing minimal disruption to other road users.

The size of your TMP will depend on the size of your event; a small local fete or fair may only be a few lines long, whereas a day-night music concert could run into several pages with detailed maps. Show all possible routes and parking areas.

You can log on to www.roadworks.org to find out if there are any roadworks on in your area – some utilities plan their big projects many months in advance, so it's worth double checking.

Don't be afraid to talk to public transport operators at an early stage too, because bus, train or taxi companies may increase the frequency of their services, if they see a commercial opportunity.

If you are planning a large-scale event, you might want to consider providing the facilities of free shuttle buses like the railway services which serve the V Festival, or set up park and ride areas.

Don't go too overboard on this, though, because in spite of the eco-lobby which is seeking to promote public transport, the majority of people still want to use their own cars.

Do you need to close a road, or change traffic flow?

It is possible, in certain circumstances, to close public roads to traffic. But this does require more foresight and advance planning, and you'll only get permission to do so with very good reason.

You'll need to involve the Local Authority and the Highways Authority at the earliest possible opportunity and justify requests for parking suspensions in your Event Safety

Management Plan and Traffic Management Plan.

The Local Authority and the Highway Authority won't even consider your request if they don't have every piece of necessary information.

Even then, bear in mind that a minimum notification time may be required which could be anywhere from SIX WEEKS TO SIX MONTHS, and there may be some charges involved.

If you are providing off road parking at your event you may be asked for a parking plan. If so, you will need to supply the specific location (street name/car park etc), the number of spaces required, plus details of who will manage this area, and how it will be stewarded.

Closing any public road, footway, footpath or verge without a lawful closure order is illegal. So, before you go down that route, ask yourself if it is really necessary. Is there a safe and practical alternative?

If there isn't, here's what you need to know, in a nutshell.

There is one piece of legislation that can be used to authorise the closure of a public highway – The Road Traffic Act 1991.

You don't have to choose – the nature of the event will do that for you:

Sport and leisure events like running races, cycling activities or triathlons involve the Road Traffic Act 1991. Under this piece of legislation, each road can only be closed once a year – so check to make sure the option is still open to you before you are too far down the line with your plans.

Events involving activities such as carnival processions, parades or gatherings for special occasions like street festivals or remembrance parades will invoke the Town Police Clauses Act 1847.

A full risk assessment, plus maps and signage proposals, and a copy of public liability insurance must be submitted before any road closure can be approved. The necessary insurance will be required.

Your road closure request will then be reviewed in consultation with the SAG Committee and Highways Authority.

ROAD CLOSURE CHECKLIST

THIS USEFUL CHECKLIST RUNS THROUGH THE FACTORS TO CONSIDER ON ROAD CLOSURES IN THE EARLIEST PLANNING STAGES

 Plan the event to take place out of peak traffic hours. (such as 7.00am to 9.30am and 4.00pm to 6.00pm)

 Are there any lessons from previous events that need to be taken into account?

 Do you have enough resources to procure and maintain the signs needed?

 Are staff competent and trained to place, maintain and remove signs?

 Have you applied for and received permission for the closure from the Local Authority or Traffic Authority?

 Have you consulted with local residents/businesses/ organisations or local disability groups about the closure?

What are the options for diversion routes? The traffic authority or the Local Authority will ultimately decide what the diversion route is, but it helps to consider it at an early stage.

Are there any motorways or major roads that might be affected? If so, a closure may well be refused or direction signing could be prohibitively expensive.

Have you consulted with local bus companies and/or emergency services regarding the closure?

Have you made any contingency plans for emergency access to your closure, for example to attend an accident?

What plans are there to remove broken down vehicles from within the closure or the diversion routes?

What plans have been made to avoid/remove vehicles already in place before the closure starts?

What plans are there to enable businesses or residents to access their property within the closure?

What training/briefings will be provided to event staff managing the closure?

ACCESS FOR ALL

Is your event sufficiently child-friendly? Have you taken into account the requirements for disabled access? And what about the needs of those visitors who may have impaired vision, or hearing, or be a little bit unsteady on their feet?

There are two very good reasons to ensure that you have taken into account arrangements for people with special needs – first, to make sure you are giving people the best visitor experience possible, and second, to make sure you comply with legislation, and don't fall foul of discrimination rules.

If you are planning a village fete, the age span and audience profile of your visitors is going to be huge – grandparents, parents and children will typically be attending.

If you are planning a music concert, on the other hand, chances are you will have a much younger demographic which brings with it a different set of challenges.

So, to a certain degree, it all comes back to knowing and understanding your target audience so that – as much as possible – you can suitably risk assess the issues and any potential residual risks you are likely to encounter.

From the moment that you publicly announce your event, it's

worthwhile considering whether you need to provide a contact point for people seeking clarification about whether you can cater for their special needs.

You might want to consider allocating a special parking zone which has the closest access point to the entrance gate, for disabled badge holders or other people with mobility issues.

If there's a likelihood of wheelchairs being on site, remember that they need more room to manoeuvre – a standard wheelchair needs around 1m x 1.5m space, while the dimensions for an electric wheelchair can be significantly larger.

You may need stewards to assist wheelchair users if the ground is unstable or has a significant incline or decent.

TOP TIP: Put yourself in the position of a visitor with mobility problems – have you got their needs covered?

There is a British Standard code of practice for the design of buildings and their approaches to meet the needs of disabled people. (If you want to check it out, search for BS 8300:2009+A1:2010)

The code looks at the design of buildings and their ability to meet the requirements of disabled people. By offering best-practice recommendations, it explains how architectural design and the built environment can help disabled people to make the most of their surroundings.

It also looks at how some facilities, such as corridors, car parks and entrances, can be designed to provide aids for the disabled, and demonstrates how additional features, including ramps, signs, lifts and guard rails, can be installed.

Remember, when you are considering wheelchair access for seated areas at an event, that many users will be accompanied by an able-bodied companion, so there needs to be sufficient space for them to sit in a designated area, together.

Make sure any wheelchair zone is well away from areas where there is a risk of a crowd surge, or bottlenecks. In the event of an emergency evacuation, could wheelchairs and pushchairs be moved swiftly, and safely?

Where toilet facilities are concerned, it's recommended that you provide one unisex cubicle for every 75 wheelchair users – properly stewarded to ensure it is not being used by others.

Local disability or accessibility groups will always be keen to give their input during your event planning phase, so don't be afraid to ask them to get involved. Their specialist expertise can save a lot of time, and trouble.

What about visitors with impaired vision? Well, bear in mind they may have trouble with cluttered or tiny signs – make sure they are clear, concise, and in well-lit areas. Are you making arrangements for the accommodation of guide dogs? People will need to know.

Again, don't be afraid to consult the experts. Groups such as The Royal National Institute for the Blind, or the British Deaf Association, can bring a perspective which you may have overlooked.

Then we come to children . . . even when an event is not aimed at youngsters, or where they may have been specifically discouraged from attending below a certain age, you're bound to find some parents bringing their kids along anyway!

Make sure that your promotional material spells out whether your event is suitable for children, and if it is, whether they need to be accompanied by an adult.

If your event is on the larger side, you must create a 'lost property' area as a matter of best practice. This can double up as a 'lost children' collection point – which must be clearly signed. Whoever is manning your public address system ought to be fully briefed.

At all of my events, if we have a lost child, through working with various police forces, we implement the following procedures:

Firstly, identify if the child is lost.

Secondly, gather as much information as possible, the name of the child, their clothing and last area where the child was seen.

We then lock down and monitor all entry and exit routes, including vehicle routes, until the child has been reunited with their parent or guardian.

Stay with the parent or guardian until the child is found, usually they are found very quickly.

Make a suitable announcement over your PA system that a child is missing within the event, giving only the essential details about the child.

Once the child is found, ensure that the parents have sufficient information to prove that they are the child's parent or guardian (for example a photo on their phone, ask the child questions etc). If you are uncertain in any circumstance regarding a lost child or parent/guardian then contact the police before handing them over.

If there are members of your events team that have been DBS (Disclosure and Barring Service) assessed then these individuals should be the people dealing with a lost or found child directly.

It is absolutely vital that any members of your team who are working with children are comprehensively briefed on all child protection issues.

Might you need to create a children's play area? If so, you will need to consider the rules around supervision, and facilities like nappy changing areas etc.

Child protection can be a particular minefield. For example, what if you have a face-painter on site, and their products bring out a reaction in a child's skin. It's important to make sure your public liability insurance cover takes on board such issues.

You can check out most of the dos and don'ts regarding young people at events by looking into The Children Act 2004, which is available online (www.legislation.gov.uk).

REMEMBER, WHEN YOU ARE CONSIDERING WHEELCHAIR ACCESS FOR SEATED AREAS AT AN EVENT, THAT MANY USERS WILL BE ACCOMPANIED BY AN ABLE-BODIED COMPANION, SO THERE NEEDS TO BE SUFFICIENT SPACE FOR THEM TO SIT IN A DESIGNATED AREA, TOGETHER.

Case Study

COHESION LIMITED

Julie Homfray wears many different hats.

Her events company, Cohesion Limited, supplies entertainment, creative ideas and marketing support, and as worked at scores of awards ceremonies, as well as private parties, company days and public events.

She currently handles the marketing and events schedule for an arts charity - an independent cinema in a converted Victorian lock factory in Wolverhampton – as well as brainstorming promotional campaigns for outdoor film festivals, and staging regular comedy nights.

Her key message to event organisers is: Immerse yourself into a diverse range of experiences to get the imagination going, prepare for all eventualities – and never, ever underestimate the value of good marketing.

She says: "Cohesion was launched in 2004. I had worked in PR, media, hospitality and artist booking, and this was an opportunity to combine all my experience and be more 'hands on' rather than completely office based.

"The biggest challenge in those early days was accepting that I couldn't sustain myself with the new business from day one.

"I had five part time jobs for the first year in addition to the business, ranging from bar work, doing 'Body Shop at Home' parties and mystery shopping! As business grew, I gradually dropped one job at a time."

So, who did she turn to for support? "Not the bank – my bank manager thought giving up my previous full time role to start a business was madness!

"My brother in law and sister are excellent business owners and inspired and advised me. I also thought back to my A-Level and Degree in Business Management for some tips, went to business start-up days and exhibitions, and read a lot of books and internet articles.

"I also volunteered on many events ranging from Birmingham Artsfest to educational events to gain more experience and contacts in new areas. I continue to do this as part of my own personal development and training."

Looking back in hindsight, Julie says the biggest mistake she made was being too afraid to charge a fair rate and not having the confidence to put wild ideas forward.

"These days I have a reputation for putting forward fresh and exciting ideas, but in the early days I really played it safe with entertainment suggestions. This has changed with age and experience."

When she was promoting the Full Beam outdoor film festival in Kidderminster, for example, she mashed up various movie themes for the poster campaign to reflect the diverse range of films on the programme, including Annie Hall, The Big Lebowski, Dirty Dancing, and Night of the Living Dead.

"In the early years, the things which helped to launch successfully and to keep going, included working from home, using a cheap-to-run car, doing as much as possible 'in house' and building friendly relationships with event teams.

"Event industry personnel move round a lot, and most new work comes from individuals I've worked with moving to new companies. I also became a fan of off-peak trains and overnight buses to cut down on expensive hotels!"

"These days I have a reputation for putting forward fresh and exciting ideas, but in the early days I really played it safe."

Julie Homfray

JULIE'S TOP THREE TIPS FOR AN EVENT ORGANISER

Don't under-budget on money and time for marketing. When you are doing a local public event, you need to keep marketing costs low, but if PR attempts don't capture press attention, or if social media isn't doing the trick, you will need to set aside some budget for advertising. Flyers are cheap and fabulous, but don't forget to allocate time to distribute them – and to work out the most effective outlets for them to be seen.

I worked with a fantastic wedding planner who taught me the importance of a Wet Weather Plan. Can your event be done in the rain? What cover, alternatives or facilities can you turn to? We worked on an outdoor event where each delegate was given a 'survival pack' which included sun cream and plastic raincoats - every single coat was used, and all the activities were able to go ahead as planned.

Every spare weekend and day, surround yourself with experiences to get your imagination going . . . go to events, collect cards and talk to people. Work for free in areas where you need the experience.

Spreading The word

You know what they say . . . all publicity is good publicity.

I'm sure there will be those out there who have reason to disagree, but when it comes to spreading the word about your event, the saying is completely true.

Because you can lay on the best event the world has ever seen, but if no-one knows about it, you've wasted your time and effort.

So don't treat the PR and marketing side of the operation as a luxury, or afterthought. It's one of the core factors on which your event will succeed, or fail, so make sure you give the task to people who understand its crucial role, and its objectives.

For starters, make sure your promotional campaign fulfils what media trainers often refers to as the 'W Formation' . . . Who, What, Where, When, and Why?

WHO: Who is the event aimed at? Who will be there providing the entertainment? And who is organising it?

WHAT: What is the purpose of the event? Is it a fundraiser for charity, perhaps, or something celebrating a particular milestone or anniversary? And what will be on offer for folk of all ages?

WHERE: Where is it being held – take into account that people may not be familiar with your choice of venue, so give full details

WHEN: When is the event being staged? Not just the date, but the times as well. If possible, try to break down the timetable into bite-sized chunks for those who may be planning to make the most of just a fleeting visit.

WHY: This is the most important question of all. Why is your event being held, and why should people turn up? If there is no compelling reason for people to feel they need to be there, apathy could start to creep in – and that's the enemy of any successful event.

So, you've got your facts and figures together and cross-checked them against the W Formation. What now? Pull together a marketing strategy which creatively plants your brand in the minds of as many people as possible, in as many different places – and aim to reach a crescendo in the three or four weeks leading up to D-Day.

WHO CAN YOU TELL?

Some events set aside a significant amount of cash for paid-for advertising, to guarantee a high profile. Most, though, will seek to achieve the majority of their PR through the many free channels which are available – if you know where to look, and how to communicate with them. They include:

NEWSPAPERS: Local papers are desperate to have local news stories laid on a plate for them these days. The print media has been through a rough time in recent years and staffing has been reduced, but research shows it's still the most trusted form of media around. So preparing professionally-written press releases which don't require huge amounts of time and editing, and answer all of those W Formation questions, is vital. Remember that newspapers are a visual media, so pull together photographs whenever you can to give a flavour of what's in store. A picture tells a thousand words – particularly when it's done shrewdly. Remember, though, that issuing a press release is no guarantee of publication; it's at the editor's discretion. The only way to guarantee that anything gets used is to pay for advertising space.

MAGAZINES: Specialist magazines will be a fabulous way to publicise your event, particularly if it has a strong theme like music, model aeroplanes etc. Most magazines will give you a forward features list explaining their terms and deadlines – it's important to remember that, unlike newspapers, magazines tend to work a long way in advance and have very early deadlines. Don't leave it too late to get in touch with them.

LOCAL RADIO: There's a BBC local station, and commercial radio network, covering virtually every inch of the UK. Make the most of them, as the BBC in particular have hours and hours of speech-based radio to fill every day. Offer up members of your organising team to go into the studio and talk about your event, and encourage any acts or attractions who are taking part to do the same. Consider the possibility of running competitions to give away tickets – that applies equally to the newspapers. See if the radio team want to bring their roadshow along to your event. If they do, you'll be assured that they want to give it plenty of on-air profile.

SOCIAL MEDIA: This part of our lives is moving so fast these days that anything I say here will probably be out of date before the book is even printed! Set yourself up with a Facebook page and a Twitter account, and start populating it regularly (not too regularly to become a nuisance, mind…). Follow and 'like' people you think could come in useful to help spread the word further. Consider whether you want to pay to boost some of your Facebook posts, which can be a cost-effective way of reaching the precise demographic of your expected audience. Just don't overdo social media, and end up becoming a nuisance on people's timelines.

A WEBSITE: Depending upon the size and regularity of your event, you might want to set up a website. This can be done relatively cheaply, or run into thousands of pounds . . . it really is up to you how much time, importance and resource you feel you should attach to it. If you want to publicise your line-up, or are hoping to make your event an annual showcase, a web presence is vital. People will expect it to be a one-stop shop for everything they need – if you are selling tickets, they'll probably expect to be able to buy them online. There are many online ticketing organisations who will handle this for you, but remember that they will want to take a share of your income.

BULLETIN BOARDS: It's not just local newspapers which have a community calendar that can list your event – contact local shops in your catchment area who will be prepared to display a poster. And make sure you include local community magazines or newsletters, which are thriving right now, and have really loyal readers. They're particularly good if your event is all about engendering community spirit.

LEAFLETS: How about printing some flyers? These can be a great way to spread the word, especially if you are on a college campus or can leave them on reception desks at local leisure venues and visitor or tourist centres etc. Don't over-clutter your flyers with words – the date, the place, and a broad idea of your event is enough, alongside contact details for folk to find out more.

POSTERS: You can put posters, signs or banners on land where the event is due to take place as long as you have the landowner's permission. If you are advertising a local event of a religious, educational, cultural, political, social or recreational nature you will not need to get advertising consent under Class

3(D) of the Advertisement Regulations. If it is being staged for commercial purposes, though, you will . . . speak to the licensing department at the Local Authority to double check. Even if you don't need consent, there are rules and regulations that have to be obeyed. They include:

The advertisement is no bigger than 0.6 of a square metre.

The advertisement is not placed any more than than 28 days before the event.

The advertisement is removed within 14 days after the end of the event.

No letters, figures, symbols or similar features on the advert are over 0.75 of a metre in height, or 0.3 metre if they are in any Area of Special Control.

The advertisement is not illuminated

No part of the advertisement is more than 4.6 metres above ground level, or 3.6 metres in an Area of Special Control.

Case Study

JOHN CHALLIS – ONLY FOOLS AND BOYCIE

John Challis is one of the nation's best known comic actors, immortalised as dodgy used car salesman Boycie in the hit comedy Only Fools and Horses. The show ran from 1981 to 2003, and when its record-breaking run finally came to an end, writer John Sullivan recognised the popularity of the character, and gave Boycie a spin-off series, The Green Green Grass, which aired for four series between 2005 and 2009.

John now goes on tour each year with a show called Only Fools and Boycie, packed with anecdotes and fascinating behind-the-scenes stories from his career.

"The show was launched as a one-off in 2012," he recalls.

"I was asked to do a show at a small theatre in Shrewsbury, which held 250. The idea was for me to be interviewed on stage and for us to show a few clips.

"We expected there to be a reasonable audience but, in fact, we sold out. We've been on the road ever since. The most shows we've done in a year is 50, though at present we're doing around half that number each year. It remains very popular."

What was the biggest challenge in those early days?

"There were two challenges. Firstly, it was a new show, so we didn't know what to expect from the audience. We didn't know whether people would turn up, whether venues would want to book it and whether fans would enjoy the format.

"The second challenge was creative. It took us 10 to 15 shows to work out what the audience really enjoyed. We continue to refine it, of course, and no two shows are ever the same. But settling on a format that people enjoyed and could relate to, took a little while."

Behind the scenes, it's far from a one-man operation. John has a promoter

who handles a lot of the details.

"For instance, he books shows, promotes shows, organises interviews and liaises with the venue on all aspects. That frees me to get on with the show and the business of Being Boycie."

Looking back in hindsight, are there any things which John would have done differently?

"We've learned as we've gone on, of course, but we've been free from any major dramas or mishaps. There have been one or two occasions when technology has failed us, though, again, my promoter fixes that. And there have been one or two shows in curious venues.

"But basically, it's been a question of putting the show out there and looking to improve night after night. I think my agent would say the challenges he has faced relate to the detail: to the percentage allowances for selling merchandise, to getting the right deals, to making sure everything's set up and organised well before I arrive at a venue and to promoting the show and building an audience.

"It's all about being diligent and being organised, from his perspective, so that I can deliver a show that the fans want."

He continues: "You learn as you go. The creative side has improved considerably as we've gone. The show sort of emerges. And as to the organisation and logistics, there are aspects that also come to the fore.

"It's about thinking ahead and making sure you've covered all bases. Is there the right insurance, were the posters sent out early enough, are there enough press interviews, is the technology in place and so on.

"Those are matters that I leave to my agent, of course, and things tend to work pretty well."

And John's top tips for budding event organisers?

"Be organised, stay calm, and remember that there's nothing that you can't fix.

"On one occasion, during a show in Liverpool, we had a computer failure, which could have ruined the show. I was standing at the front of the stage at the time and was completely unaware of what was going on.

"My agent tip-toed off stage, ran round the back, fixed the parts that had

failed and within five minutes everything was fine. There was another example of that at a different venue.

"So stay calm, keep the show on the road and – as Dad's Army would say – don't panic."

John has worked with Jonathan at more than 10 events and said: "He's always been charming, professional, polite and exhibited high levels of skill. He earns the trust of participants, exhibitors and artists, helping us to feel comfortable at events for which he holds responsibility. He is both highly regarded and highly recommended."

"Be organised, stay calm, and remember that there's nothing that you can't fix."

John Challis

Case Study

YARRINGTON

Yarrington is a multi award-winning marketing, design, video and event management company, providing services to clients across Britain.

Formed in 1997, the Midlands-based company has worked with a succession of top-branded organisations on awards nights, conferences, product launches, exhibitions . . . and much, much more.

Managing Director Mark Allsop says: "Great events don't happen by accident. They're the result of lots of hard work and, above all, planning. Plan each and every detail. Then plan them again.

"Make lists and endless notes, build spreadsheets and cross reference them. Refine your ideas and keep track of each element. Leave nothing to chance."

His advice to organisers is to never assume anything is under control, until you can prove that you are right …

"If a supplier has promised a delivery, don't expect that it will automatically happen. If a printer has promised your menus for a certain time, don't believe it until they arrive.

"If you don't understand something a supplier is telling you (for example about an amazing piece of technical equipment) ask questions until you do."

Mark adds: "Events can be outrageously stressful, especially for the non-specialist. So remember that the world will keep on turning and tomorrow will surely dawn, even if something doesn't turn out the way you wanted.

"It's only an event and there's no need to have a meltdown over it. It's a fact that if your guests weren't expecting something, then they won't notice if it's not there.

"For example, the amazing balloon arch you planned for the entrance that failed to materialise won't be a point of ridicule if guests weren't aware that it was supposed to be there."

And he says: "Work with event professionals. Don't for a moment believe that you, an amateur, could possibly know all there is to know about events just because you fancy having a go.

"People work in this industry all their lives and are hugely experienced and successful. Working with them will take the vast majority of the stress away and allow you to actually enjoy the event.

"Don't lose your cool. However stressful things become always be polite. Catering staff, audio visual crew, meet and greet teams are all trying to make the event a success as well. They really don't work harder or faster when somebody starts shouting at them. In most instances the opposite happens and you will just look foolish.

"Don't drink before, during or after your event. Ever. If the client offers you a drink for all your hard work, politely decline. Adrenaline and alcohol are poor bedfellows."

Mark's final piece of advice is this: "Keep your client informed with regular updates and meetings. Be clear and don't fudge difficult conversations.

"If budgets change, you'll need to explain the situation sooner rather than later. And talking of budgets . . . make sure you get paid!"

"Don't lose your cool. However stressful things become always be polite. People really don't work harder or faster when somebody starts shouting at them. In most instances the opposite happens and you will just look foolish."

Mark Allsop

Mark Allsop of Yarrington, right, receives the company's latest award

Firm Foundations

How long does it take to build your average house? Three, four months perhaps?

When it comes to putting up structures at your public event, it has to be done in a matter of hours – but must still be built to last, ultra-safe, and capable of withstanding a double barrage . . . from the unpredictable paying punters, and the even more unpredictable British weather.

So don't underestimate the time and painstaking planning which needs to go into setting up every single structure which will be on your showground.

Chances are, you'll have at least one, and probably more of these involved in your event:

Marquees

Stages

Temporary seating

Wooden or plastic shelters

PA systems

Advertising hoardings

TV and video screens

Crowd management barriers

These two photos were taken just 2 seconds apart
and show the moment a stand collapsed in Brazil.

Pictures: YouTube

The collapse of any structure, in such a confined space where there are likely to be considerable crowds of people, can have devastating consequences. People can be fatally injured.

So, make sure you've not only picked the right kind of material for each structure, but you've also positioned your structures in areas of least potential danger. Contractors need to have a knowledge and understanding of the particular challenges involved in event work, and must employ an appropriately trained workforce. Always ask for certification.

History is littered with tragic stories of structural faults with temporary spectator areas at large events.

If you take a look at YouTube, you'll find shocking footage of the day that over 100 people were hurt – 22 critically – when part of a metal stand gave way at the Quatro Pontes race track in Brazil back in 2010.

Authorities said structural faults were almost certainly to blame for the collapse – imagine the litigation that you'd open yourself up to in circumstances like this.

There was another notorious accident in Indiana in August 2011, when a gust of wind hit the roof at the State Fair, causing it collapse. The structure landed on a huge crowd of spectators, killing seven people and injuring 58.

One of the reasons for this is because the rules surrounding temporary demountable structures fall outside the usual civil and structural engineering regulations.

Temporary structures, as previously mentioned, may have to be designed by a competent person, usually a Structural Engineer.

Remember it is also likely that once you are building temporary structures they will come under the Construction (Design and Management) Regulations 2015 and other associated legislation.

If in doubt, check out legislation such as The Work At Height Regulations of 2005, or the Management of Health and Safety At Work Regulations of 1999. The Health and Safety Executive will have a field-day if you've tried to cut corners.

So what sort of factors do you have to consider? Well, for starters, if your event is outdoors, how firm and flat is the ground and will it withstand any point loads or loadings onto the ground? If the heavens open, will it drain quickly, or might foundations become unstable in soft earth?

Are there any services within the ground that could prove to be a void area or pit, causing the structure to be unstable?

Then there are wind loading and the effects of climatic conditions to consider. Snow in winter, flash floods in summer, all will have an effect on a temporary structure.

Always consider the audience and support of a competent Structural Engineer for any significant temporary structure.

Consider, too, that there may be underground cables or pipes that need to be avoided – as well as overhead wires which you'll need to steer well clear of.

Make sure that the Structural Engineer is called once your structures have been built and they provide you with the correct "sign off" procedures or certification to ensure that seating structures, or any other load-bearing equipment, have been tested to ensure they can take the weight.

If you are erecting marquees or large gazeboes for your event, the company who erects these should work with a suitable structural engineer to provide this information.

Remember that the marquees will need to be suitably fire rated and also signed off when complete.

Never underestimate the weight of lighting rigs, projection screens, or sound systems. And make sure every advertising banner is fastened down strong enough to withstand the strongest gust of wind – and placed, where possible, in more sheltered parts of your event.

TOP TIP: Make sure all temporary structures have been checked over by an expert before the public are admitted to your event – and know what the law demands of you as the event organiser.

Many of the structures at your event will be deemed a residual risk – particularly where lighting or electricity is involved. So make sure they are fenced off with crowd control barriers, and suitable signage and protected against the hands of a small child.

Well-placed barriers are not just a useful tool to protect hazardous areas, they are also perfect to direct visitors or to segregate different attractions.

But poorly-placed barriers can themselves create a hazard, particularly during an emergency.

The type of barrier or fencing you use is important, and it needs to be fit for purpose – for example, a single rope barrier might not be right if there are lots of small children around, and very sturdy metal structures will be required if there's a possibility of a crowd surge at a music concert. These structures or barriers may need to be suitable or demountable in the event of a crowd surge to prevent a crush injury.

If you have food concession stands on your site, it's worth contacting the Public Protection Officers for your Local Authority to ensure you are meeting their rules.

You can also find structural and legal advice regarding food businesses at the website food.gov.uk.

Case Study

EQUESTRIAN DOUBLE-BILL

Alan Beaumont Management is a Cheshire-based company founded in 1997. It has a proud record of creating events that are admired and run as efficiently and cost-effectively as possible.

The company has delivered a string of top events, including Bolesworth International, the four-day equestrian spectacular in 6,000 acres of castle grounds near Chester, and the Liverpool International Horse Show, held at the city's Echo Arena.

The Liverpool International Horse Show featured international show jumping competitions with some of the world's top riders across three action packed days, with riders competing for a total prize fund of £200,000.

Each show also featured exciting displays and music, with food and drink outlets situated around the arena, with a walk-in bistro style restaurant and luxurious champagne bar alongside the collecting ring in the BT Convention Centre, linked to the Echo Arena by a covered atrium.

The BT Convention Centre also housed a Shopping Village with outlets retailing high-end clothing, equestrian accessories, giftwares, fine foods and beautiful things for the home.

So, a big logistical challenge then?

Alan Beaumont says: "Bolesworth International was first launched in 2008 to promote International show jumping in the UK. The biggest challenge in those early days was finance, and we turned to industry experts for advice and support.

"Looking back in hindsight, the biggest mistake we made was not planning for growth adequately.

"And if we could have done anything differently in the planning stages, it

would have been employing more staff."

For Alan, event management is multi-faceted. It includes liaison with Local Authorities (health and safety, environmental, police, fire, ambulance and traffic), plus hospitality units, public and private catering units, public and private bars.

It also covers public address and sound systems, security, stewarding and crowd control, veterinary cover, contractor vetting, plus publicity and marketing, and medical cover (both for the public and competitors).

But it doesn't end there. Other considerations include waste management, trade stand and exhibitor management, helicopter management, hotel accommodation, and logistics.

Alan's top tips to a budding event organiser are based around three key areas. *First, make sure your financial planning is sound and realistic. Second, make sure you invest for the future if you plan to make your event a regular on the calendar. And third, never underestimate any of the aspects involved in staging a successful event.*

Tickets, Sponsors and Stallholders

Turnover is vanity, profit is sanity.

The business guru who coined that catchy phrase hit the nail right on the head.

It's no good charging gung-ho ahead with the organisation of your event until you have thought carefully about how to maximise your potential income streams.

Here are just three of the questions you should be asking yourselves, right at the beginning of the process:

Do we charge for admission, or let people in free? If we're charging, what's the pricing structure?

Are there any opportunities for attracting sponsorship? And if so, how do we make ourselves appealing to a sponsor?

Could we charge stallholders and/or caterers to attend? And if so, how much?

It's crucial to be realistic. You're far better off to underestimate your income, and over-exaggerate your running costs, than to do it the other way round!

TICKET SALES

If you've decided that people should pay to attend your event, you need to be clear in your mind about how they get hold of tickets, where they should be marketed, and how much they should cost.

You might want to give people some kind of 'early bird' discount offer to encourage visitors not to leave their purchases to the last minute. This is a good way of gauging early interest.

Offering discounted tickets to groups is also a great way of shifting large volumes.

Make the most of the online world. Most of us are sending emails every day, so include an event promotion in your email signature, or change your Facebook and Twitter cover photos, to point people towards the ticketing service for your event. It's free, and can be very effective.

There are various online ticketing websites available, like Eventbrite, or TicketSource (other brands are available!), which offer a free internet-based box office service. They are relatively easy to use, and understand – all you have to do is register for an account. These operators do take a small percentage of each ticket sale, typically around 3%, as commission.

Think carefully about that quote from Lord Sebastian Coe at the start of the book. Have you come up with a catchy name for your event which explains what it's all about? Strong branding will boost your ticket sales.

Ask an innocent bystander to give you their views on your logo, event name, or poster? Do they understand what the event is all about, and was it easy to grasp? If the answer is no, you might need to go back to the drawing board I'm afraid.

Consider some sort of VIP package. It's amazing how many people will pay a premium if they think it will guarantee a more luxurious experience – if people have decided they want to come to your event, they'll often be prepared to do what it takes to make it the best possible occasion.

A VIP ticket might allow an earlier entrance time, give access to a private bar or dining area – as long as it has a clear added value, in an aspirational kind of way, that bit is really up to you.

So, when should you put your tickets on sale? There's no hard and fast rule, but the popular wisdom is that the more expensive your event, the earlier you need it to have your tickets on sale, to start the revenue coming in – and give you some financial peace of mind too!.

V Festival, for example, typically puts its tickets on sale from mid February, for the event which is staged towards the end of August.

For free-to-attend smaller events, or those with nominal ticket prices, there's no need to panic if sales are sluggish, so potentially no need to aggressively push sales quite so early.

Having said that, you should always be offering some sort of compelling incentive to buy early. "Book early to avoid disappointment" – that's not what you need to say, but it's what you need to make people think.

Talking to groups who have organised similar events can provide a really helpful indication of likely costs and income, and where to pitch your ticket prices.

FINDING A SPONSOR

Why did Barclays fork out an eye-watering £120 million to sponsor the English football Premier League for three seasons?

What made Vodafone think Formula One motor racing team McLaren was worth $75 million of its money for just one season?

And how come gaming companies are falling over themselves to add their names to sporting competitions from snooker and darts to football, cricket and rugby?

The answer: In their eyes, sponsorship is seen as a much more cost-effective and targeted form of brand awareness than traditional adverts or billboards, which simply shout about how much better you are than your competition.

They have the 'so what!' factor these days. The public takes the attitude that the advertisers would say that, because they're paying for it. We're more cynical than we've ever been...

Sponsorship is slightly different. Every event will have a specific mix of people in attendance – and if they are a company's target market, and the brand is confident in the event's reputation, why wouldn't they want to slap their name all over it?

Sounds easy, doesn't it? Well, it's not. Potential sponsors will want to know exactly how you can guarantee to attract the right kind of audience (backed up by a detailed marketing plan), and how heavily their brand will be promoted beforehand, and displayed on the day.

It's closely tied in with the event's PR strategy – sponsors will want to see what sort of exposure you are going to give them, in return for them endorsing your event with what is, hopefully, a powerful and respected name.

Sponsorship can come on almost any level. It might mean simply giving a company a larger stand, an enhanced editorial profile on the website or in the programme, or allowing them to hand out flyers. If they're a headline sponsor, on the other hand, they might have their name included in the title of the event, and their logo across all marketing material.

Don't under-value a headline sponsorship. Bear in mind that a company would expect to pay up to £2,000 just for a single-page advertisement in a local daily newspaper. Could your event give them 10 times the exposure, not to mention potential exclusivity, and association with a 'feelgood factor' event? Food for thought.

Spending a large part of their advertising budget as a sponsor or vendor at an event is increasingly being seen by companies as a much wiser strategy, bringing a greater return on investment.

If you are planning a relatively locally-based event which is raising cash for charity, go to the town's largest or best known employer. Chances are, they'll have a budget set aside for what's called Corporate Social Responsibility (CSR), meaning you'll tick one of their boxes.

Sponsorship that involves hospitality always appeals to companies too. Why? Because it gives them the chance to network with a captive audience of potential new clients, or to treat some of the most valued existing customers to consolidate their relationships.

Don't make the mistake, though, of feeling that sponsors will just come knocking on your door. They may not know about the good causes you'll be raising money for, or the irresistible line-up that you are planning. They won't be as excited about your event as you are – they'll need to be sold into your vision.

You have to earn your sponsorship, and appreciate that your sponsor will want to see exactly why it's worth them placing their brand into your hands.

CHARGING STALLHOLDERS

Sometimes, an event organiser will look at their overall running costs, and feel they can get the entire figure covered by fees from stallholders.

That way, anything they earn on the day is going straight into the profit pot, removing a lot of the risk – not to mention sleepless nights.

Having the right blend of stallholders at an event can greatly increase its attraction to a wider audience. There's nothing worse than hearing people saying 'There's nothing to do' when they arrive.

So, think about the sort of stalls that will offer something for all the family, from bouncy castles to local produce stalls, climbing walls, funfairs, cake stalls, face painting . . . the list goes on, and on.

Usually, you'd either charge a fixed rate for a table or stall, or simply ask the stallholder for a percentage of their sales on the day. It depends on your attitude to risk – do you prefer to know exactly what's coming into your bank account ahead of the day, or want to gamble on earning even more if your event is a success?

Either way, you may want to consider asking them for a deposit to cover yourself in the event of a late cancellation.

Make sure that your stallholders are aware of set up times, risk and safety rules, and on-site facilities, and the timetable for breaking down their stalls and leaving the site.

Try not to book too many similar stalls which may be high street competitors – they won't thank you for that - and make sure you have a clear site plan so it's not a free-for-all seeking to grab the best plot.

Even Sunday morning car boot sales have pre-booked plots and sophisticated floorplans these days!

TOP TIP: Don't underestimate your value to potential sponsors – but be prepared to work hard to prove that your event is beneficial to their brand.

Case Study
ENERGIZE COMMUNITY SPORTS AWARDS

The Energize community sports awards have attracted some of the biggest names in British sport – from football legend Peter Shilton to cricket record-breaker Graham Gooch, rugby world cup winner Neil Back, and Olympic competitors such as Sharron Davies, Mark Foster, Katherine Merry, Steve Backley and Tessa Sanderson. They are organised by one of the 45 county sports partnerships in the UK.

Energize marketing manager Tamsin Foster took five minutes to answer a few of our quickfire questions, and offer up some useful tips:

When was your event first launched, and why?

"The first event was in 2007. We launched it because we felt local grassroots sport wasn't recognised at a county level at that point, and the ethos of the event – recognising and celebrating community sport and the people that make it happen – fitted with our aims and objectives as a county sports

The Energize Sports Awards. Opposite page, rugby legend Neil Back MBE speaking at the awards cermony and above Olympic swimmer Sharron Davies with some of the winners

partnership. It was seen as a good opportunity to raise the profile of local sport and of Energize at the same time."

What was the biggest challenge in those early days?

"The first couple of years were more difficult in terms of getting the quantity and quality of nominations in for the awards. It was also harder to fill the venue and sell the tickets, because we needed to establish the event's profile.

"Media engagement took a bit more work in the early days too."

Who did you turn to, for advice and support?

"A number of people helped to grow the event. The first year a local PR company gave some support in terms of seeking a sponsor, media engagement and general event management. There was also a small committee involved in organising the event who had a range of advice according to their skills and areas of expertise."

Looking back in hindsight, what was the biggest mistake you made?

"Taking for granted the sponsor we had in the first two years (we had a headline sponsor which helped to offset some of our running costs) and what was involved in managing that relationship in order to maintain the partnership with the event."

If you could have done anything differently in the planning stages, what would it have been?

"Consider it an all year round planning cycle from the outset. In the early days we tended to spend time planning the event in certain months, where it's actually a continuous cycle. Also, we would have got our sponsorship offer properly established in the early days."

If you could give a budding event organiser any top tips what would they be?

"Plan well in advance – the event happens on one day, but the planning cycle is continuous. Look after your partners, sponsors and supporters. Ensure they're getting what they want and need from the event / relationship. Think of it as a partnership rather than them just handing you over money. Stay true to your event, never losing sight of who or what it's for, or about."

"Plan well in advance – the event happens on one day, but the planning cycle is continuous. Look after your partners, sponsors and supporters. Ensure they're getting what they want and need from the event / relationship."

Tamsin Foster

Case Study

UNIVERSITY OF BIRMINGHAM PRE-OLYMPIC TRAINING CAMP – VOLUNTEERS

As the Sports Project Manager at the University of Birmingham, part of Sue Briggs' portfolio included coordinating international athlete and squad camps before major competitions and she was fortunate enough to be the co-ordinator for the Jamaican Track and Field Pre Olympic Games Training Camp, prior to the London 2012 Olympics.

She said: "The University of Birmingham had worked strategically with Birmingham City Council to secure the Jamaican Olympic Association's commitment to training in Birmingham prior to the Games and a key part of our delivery plan was the use of volunteers for a variety of roles.

Volunteers made this event, without them the Camp would not have be the success it was.

"The Camp involved 60+ athletes, coaches and team management, including high profile names such as Usain Bolt, Yohan Blake and Shelley-Ann Fraser-Pryce, staying at the University's conference facilities and training on site for a 10 day period. The principle of the Camp was to provide a 'home-away-from-home' where athletes could train away from the gaze of media interest and prepare for one of the most important times of their athletic careers whilst also being able to relax and enjoy some of the sights Birmingham had to offer."

Scope

"From the start we identified that volunteers would be needed for a variety of roles. We starting with a scoping exercise to clearly define what we did and didn't want volunteers to be involved in. We had to be mindful of the sensitive nature of the involvement with the athletes and needed to ensure that all roles and tasks were focused on delivering a quality camp set around the Camp Principles. Roles ranged from assisting our security team ensuring athlete privacy was maintained at all times, setting up the athletes training facilities to ensure equipment was to hand, escorting athletes to training facilities, being tour guides, and assisting with general one off tasks. We recruited volunteers from across a spectrum of courses and year groups, some of who we clearly identify as having the skills to be team leaders. Almost all of our volunteers had had some previous experience of volunteering at sports events but what we required the most was volunteers who could display integrity and discretion and an ability to adaptable."

Public Face

"We were asking for volunteers to work with the Camp for a two-week period, 24 hours a day 7 days a week. We are offering something unique to the Jamaican track and Field team and our volunteers had to understand that they were public face of the Camp. They were the people that athletes and team management would interact with, they were the ones who would appear in the paparazzi shots, they were the ones who would represent the University and the City Council when out and about. In short, the success of the Camp was to rely entirely on the quality of the volunteers."

Recruit

"We advertised via the University's website for volunteers, but also looked to key community groups to find suitable volunteers who might be able to give us cultural insight to the team and athletes. All potential volunteers were interviewed and underwent a thorough screening process. From the start, we had to be very careful about managing expectations. We were looking for people who had offered their services for genuine reasons, not just because they liked athletics and wanted to spend the day with the team! We also required people who could work under their own initiative, were willing to work unsociable hours and were very obviously team players."

Induct & Support

"Clarity on roles is very important. The induction process enabled us to be very clear on what a volunteer was going to do and what they are not going to do. Who did they report do, what are their boundaries/protocols (so important when working with high profile athletes). We also wanted to reassure the volunteers that they had a large network and support team around them if they felt that something wasn't going to plan. Each volunteer was allocated a team with a team leader, who then reported to a member of staff (Volunteer Development Manager), so everyone had support for any issues that arose during the Camp. There were daily briefings with each team and all team leaders ensuring the key points and timetable for the day (which was ever changing) was known to all."

Reward

"Every volunteer was given a t-shirt and waterproof, uniquely designed for the Camp. However, the real rewards lay in the 'money can't buy' experiences for many of the volunteers. Who can say they have played dominos with Usain Bolt, gone to the cinema with some of the greatest athletes of our time, or indeed just sat and chatted about what it is like to compete on the international stage over a cup of tea? These are memories that will stay with the volunteers forever. As many of our volunteers were young (up to 22), the experiences they gained also enabled them to have great CVs on graduation and would have certainly been a talking point for any prospective employer."

"The value of volunteers cannot be underestimated and any event organiser should invest time thinking about how to recruit, deploy and support volunteers. Volunteers will make or break your event and having a plan for them from the out-set will make your event run much more smoothly."

Sue Briggs

About Online Safety Solutions Ltd

I never intended to write this book as an advertisement for Online Safety Solutions Ltd – fortunately I do not have to, as recommendations from our clients come to us on a weekly basis. I consider myself very fortunate to be able to work with such a terrific team of staff.

Online Safety Solutions Ltd are one of the UK's leading Risk and Safety Management Consultancies, specialising within the Events, Historical and Heritage Buildings and Construction Sectors, working both nationally and internationally.

We can provide a practicable, common sense approach to either an event, a project or a building.

Please visit our website: www.oss-hs.com

or email: info@online-safetysolutions.co.uk

or telephone: 0845 555 2010.

Stay safe and have a wonderful event

Jonathan

ACKNOWLEDGEMENTS

The author and publisher would like to thank the following companies, and individuals, for their support and assistance in producing this guide:

Alan Beaumont Management
Cohesion Limited – Julie Homfray
Energize County Sports Partnership – Tamsin Foster
Jigsaw Medical Services – Richard McManus
John Challis
Light House Media Centre, Wolverhampton
Liz Hobbs Group Limited
Nativemonster.co.uk
Rachel Jones Public Relations
Shrewsbury Food Festival – Beth Heath
Southwater Event Group – Vikki Kennedy
University Of Birmingham – Sue Briggs
The Midland News Association
The Knights of the Damned – Justin Pearson
The Jockey Club – Epsom
V Festival team
Yarrington Limited – Mark Allsop

REFERENCES

The Event Safety Guide – Health & Safety Executive
Guide to Health, Safety and Welfare at Pop Concerts and Similar Events – Health and Safety Commission / Home Office / The Scottish Office
Legislation.gov.uk